Determinants of
Mental Health

A SOCIOECONOMIC PERSPECTIVE

Ramesh N. Bhardwaj Ph.D.
PROFESSOR GEORGE BROWN COLLEGE

CONTRIBUTOR: ATUL BHARDWAJ FREELANCER DATA ANALYST

ACKNOWLEDGMENT AND DISCLAIMER

We thank Dr. Nikola Grujich of Sunnybrook Hospital, Toronto, Ontario, who introduced us to the collaborative care model of mental health. This study is an extension of our learning from Dr. Grujich. We also owe thanks to Megan Snair, our editor, who provided us with valuable suggestions and guidance at many places. We, however, take the full responsibility for remaining errors in this manuscript.

Due care has been taken to cite and credit the published research papers and sources used in this study. Please bring to the authors' notice any discrepancy or omission in this regard. We apologize for any inadvertent errors or omissions. The opinions expressed here are solely those of the authors and do not reflect the views of the organizations to which they belong.

TERMS AND ACRONYMS USED

ASR: Age-standardized rates
AUD: Alcohol Use Disorder
CSDH: The Commission on Social Determinants of Health
DALYs: Disability-Adjusted Life Year (DALY)
DUD: Drug Use Disorder
EPL: Employment Protection Legislation
ESPAD: European School Survey Project on Alcohol and Other Drugs
GBD: Global Burden of Disease
HED: heavy episodic drinking
HICs: high-income countries
ILO: International Labor Organization
LMIC: Low- and middle-income countries
M&SUD: mental and substance use disorder
MTF: Monitoring the Future
NCDs: non-communicable diseases
NEET: not in education, employment and training
OECD: Organization for Economic Co-operation and Development
PCP: primary care physicians
PLSR: partial least square regression
PLS: partial least square
SAMHSA: Substance Abuse and Mental Health Services Administration

SUD: Substance Use Disorder

UNODC: United Nations Office on Drug Control

WHO: World Health Organization WHO's Classification of World Regions

AFR: African Region

EMR: Eastern Mediterranean Region

EUR: European Region

SEAR: South-East Asia Region

WPA: Western Pacific Region

YLD: years lived with disability

YLL: years of life lost

EXECUTIVE SUMMARY

The World Health Organization (WHO) defines mental health as a state of well-being in which every individual realizes his or her own potential, can cope with the normal stresses of life, can work productively and fruitfully, and is able to contribute to her or his community. However, the world is far off this state of mental health and well-being. Worldwide evidence confirms: high onset of neuropsychiatric disorders before the age of 14; mental disorders as the leading causes of world- wide disability in young people; mental illness along with substance use contributing to many suicides; and both in combination acting as high risk factors for other diseases (such as human immunodeficiency virus, cardiovascular disease, diabetes, and viceversa). People with mental dis- orders experience significant disability and negative impact on quality of life, greatly affecting their families and communities.

Prevention of mental disorders along with the measures that promote mental well-being are considered evidence-based and cost-effective strategies. Prevention measures require addressing the root causes of these disorders. Research shows that mental disorders have etiologies that are largely multifactorial, involving complex interactions between genetic, neurobiological, and environmental factors. There is now robust evidence that mental health and many common mental disorders are shaped to a great extent by the social, economic, and physical environments in which people live, grow, and work. Adopting broad-based societal interventions that improve and facilitate access to vital economic resources, educational opportunities, and gainful employment hold a great promise of containing the prevalence of psychiatric disorders.

The objective of this paper is to investigate these socioeconomic impediments that contribute to the unabated prevalence of mental health disorders across OECD countries. This study, using the partial least square approach on cross-sectional data, ascertained the relative role of the structural factors such as wealth distribution inequality, income quintile ratio, youth poverty, employment precarity, median rental cost burden on bottom quintile, and the percentage of children with single-parent households. In addition to these structural factors, the study also highlighted the barriers posed by the lagging health care system of countries; both developed and selected developing nations. Further, due to the strong connection between mental illness and the use of psychoactive substances, the present study has also examined the growing risk of substance-use disorder among the youth population. The disease burden of mental illness has been analyzed with a primary focus on children, adolescents, and young adults. Empirical evidence of disease burden by age-group highlight the need for increased public health attention on early formative years.

Since social inequalities are known to be associated with increased risk of many common mental and substance-use disorders, population-based preventive actions are suggested that address the fundamental causes of mental illness. For interventions to be effective, medical and evidence-based behavioral research suggests public policies and programs focus on a healthy start to life and target the needs of people at critical periods throughout their lifetime. It is well acknowledged by leading health organizations and experts that a life-course approach to mental health is needed that builds on the interaction of multiple pro- motive, protective, and risk factors throughout people's lives.

Table of Contents

EXECUTIVE SUMMARY —6

1. INTRODUCTION: PROBLEM STATEMENT —9
2. THE PREVALENCE AND DISEASE BURDEN OF MENTAL DISORDERS —13
3. SOCIOECONOMIC DETERMINANTS OF MENTAL HEALTH (CSDH FRAMEWORK) —28
4. EMPIRICAL ESTIMATES OF THE SOCIO-ECNOIC DETERMINATES OF THE PREVALENCE OF MENTAL DISORDERS —43

APPENDIX TO CH 4: PARTIAL LEAST SQUARE REGRESSION APPROACH —66

5. MENTAL HEALTH CARE: CHALLENGES AND RESOURCES GAPS IN COUNTRIES —68
6. SUBSTANCE USE DISORDERS AND MENTAL ILLNESS —72
7. MENTAL AND SUBSTANCE-USE DISORDERS IN BRICS —87
8. PUBLIC HEALTH POLICY: EVIDENCE BASED PREVENTIVE INTERVENTIONS —98
9. SUMMARY AND RECOMMENDATIONS —107

REFERENCES —114

END NOTES —173

1. INTRODUCTION: PROBLEM STATEMENT

Mental, neurologic, and substance-use disorders[1] are prevalent in all regions of the world and are major contributors to morbidity and premature death. Their economic and social burden is expressed in terms of disability-adjusted life years (DALYs).[2] This metric is calculated as the sum of the number of years lived with a disability (YLDs) plus the number of years of life lost (YLLs) due to premature death. Mental and substance-use disorders (MSUD) have been shown to be responsible for 22.9% of worldwide YLDs, making them the leading cause (Whiteford et al. 2015). The estimates prepared by Vigo, Thornicroft, and Atun (2016) place mental illness a runaway first place in global burden of disease in terms of YLDs, and level with cardiovascular and circulatory diseases in terms of DALYs. These authors found that the global YLDs in 2013 from mental illness were three to five times greater than the disability associated with all infectious diseases, four times than for all injuries combined, eight times the disability associated with all cardiovascular and circulatory diseases, and 24 times the disability associated with all cancers. The global cost of mental disorders, which was estimated to be approximately $2.5 trillion in 2010, is projected to increase by 240% ($6 trillion) by 2030 (Marquez and Saxena 2016).

The highest proportion of total mental disorder DALYs occur in people aged 10–29 years, which represents 27% of the world population (Gore et al. 2011; Whiteford et al. 2015). Mental health issues affect 10 to 20% of children and adolescents worldwide, accounting for 15 to 30% of DALYs lost during the first three decades of life (Kieling et al. 2011). OECD country studies have documented that mental health was responsible for between one-third and one-half of all long-term sickness and disability among the working-age population (OECD, 2015d). This poses a grave concern since mental sickness lowers education outcomes and increases early drop out from school (OECD, 2015d). Most tragically, poor mental health is a significant factor in suicides and increases the likelihood of drug and alcohol abuse, which can lead to risky sexual behaviors and increased road injuries. Strong evidence indicates that people in lower socio-economic status are at a higher risk of mental disorders (Saraceno and Saxena, 2005a).[3]

Advances in neurosciences and behavioral medicines have revealed that mental and behavioral disorders are the result of *genetics plus social environment factors* (WHO, 2001; Wilkinson and Marmot, 2003). While genetic and biological factors (e.g., attributes that persons are endowed with at birth including chromosomal abnormalities, maladaptive personality, and intellectual disability caused by prenatal exposure to alcohol or oxygen deprivation at birth) contribute to various kinds of behavioral problems, social-economic determinants, on the other hand, are considered to exert additional dominant influence. Social and environmental factors influence genetic determinants of health and illness through gene-by-environment interactions, that is, through epigenetic mechanisms (Crompton and Shim, 2015).

In the near future, low-income countries and other developing countries[4] are projected to experience a higher burden of mental disorders, as these heavily populated countries are undergoing demographic and epidemiologic transition. Currently, these countries are facing mounting pressure on resources to cope with the double burden of communicable and non-communicable diseases (NCDs) (Boutayeb 2006). In China and India, which together jointly account for 38% of the world population, the burden of mental, neurological, and substance-use disorders (SUDs) is forecast to increase by 10% and 23%, respectively, between 2013 and 2025 (Charlson et al. 2016). Unchecked mental disorders and population level risk factors can lead to several undesired but preventable social and economic effects—viz., functional impairment, disability, and increased use of health services. What's more, untreated mental illness may result in several risks—living in poverty, lower educational attainment, teenage childbearing, domestic violence, and comorbid chronic medical conditions (Kohn et al. 2004). Action on such social determinants of health is necessary (Marmot 2005) in order to de-escalate the incidence, prevalence, and recurrence of mental disorders. The present study uses cross-sectional data and attempts to analyze the social determinants of mental health that accounted for variations in the prevalence of mental disorders among OECD countries.

PLAN OF THE STUDY

The present study of mental health determinants is organized into the following sections. In section 2, some general trends are outlined about the global burden of mental disorders and accompanying socioeconomic consequences. Section 3 presents a brief view of the WHO's framework of the structural determinants of health and lists the selected potential predictors utilized in our empirical estimation in the next section. The empirical findings are reported and discussed in section 4. Section 5 examines challenges and gaps facing health care systems of countries in meeting timely and adequate health care needs of the population. Section 6 deals with the growing menace of substance abuse among youth in high income countries, and its impact on their mental health. In section 7, the experience of BRICSs[5] is briefly outlined in respect of mental and substance use disorders facing youth. Prevention strategy aimed at removing structural obstacles to mental health is outlined in section 8. Finally, the study concludes in section 9.

2. THE PREVALENCE AND DISEASE BURDEN OF MENTAL DISORDERS

Mental disorders, when viewed in terms of prevalence[6] and the burden of disease, are among the greatest public health challenges in the world today. High prevalence of mental and substance use disorders (M&SUD) is becoming a significant source of disability across the globe, and there is a call for policies that shield people against probable risk factors. Since young people aged 15 to 24 are more likely to experience mental illness and/or SUDs than any other age group, the social and economic burden in the forms of educational failures, suicides, juvenile crimes, deaths and morbidity presents complex challenges for every country.

The following subsections provide evidence on the prevalence and disease burden of M&SUD over time for world regions.

2.1 PREVALENCE ESTIMATES

The aggregate lifetime prevalence of common mental disorders was estimated at 29.2% from 85 surveys undertaken across 39 countries (Steel et al., 2014; Whiteford, Degenhardt, Rehm, Baxter, & Ferrari, 2013. Evidence from several large-scale mental health surveys confirm that common mental disorders are highly prevalent globally, affecting people across all regions of the world (Steel et al 2014). In a systematic review and meta-analysis, Steel et al (2014) found that that approximately one in five persons experienced a common mental disorder within a 12-month period, indicated by 155 general population surveys undertaken in 59 countries.[7]

Overall the data indicate, as shown in Table 1 below, that the prevalence of mental disorders has not changed over time despite our improved understanding of the risk factors. Studies indicate that the majority of people with disorders do not receive treatment (Kohn et al. 2004, Kessler et al. 2005, Patel et al 2010, Whiteford et al. 2013) either due to insufficient resources and neglect of mental health issues in a country's health care system, or largely due to countries' failures to address the root causes, such socioeconomic inequalities and gene-environmental risks interactions (Jaffee & Price, 2007, Albrecht et al., 2007). In addition to the role of distal macro factors, proximate factors such as parental roles and social relations in the community environment can act as risk or protective factors closer to the individual. School-aged children and adolescents spend most of their days at school, which involves interacting with their peers and teachers. Social relations and school environment matter a great deal in school children's mental health. Adolescents who experience bullying (including cyber bullying or traditional bullying) as perpetrators and/or victims are more likely to have depressive and anxiety symptoms, low self-esteem, feelings of loneliness, and lost interest in activities (OECD 2018).

High prevalence of mental disorders causes considerable suffering and disease burden. In terms of DALYs, mental disorders rank almost as high as cardiovascular diseases and respiratory diseases and surpass all different types of cancer and human immunodeficiency virus (HIV) (Ustiin 1999). In 2016, the DALYs related to M&SUD contributed around 23% of the total DALYs attributable to NCDs (GBD 2016 Dis- ease and Injury Incidence and Prevalence Collaborators, Lancet 2017).

Table 1. Global Mental Disorders: Incidence, Prevalence and Disease Burden: 2016

Disease	Incidence thousands	Prevalence thousands	Disease Burden (YLD) thousands	Percentage Change in YLD 2006-2016	Percentage change in age-standardized rates between 2006 and 2016
Mental and substance use disorders[8]	410091	1111147	150476	12.9	-1.4
Depressive disorders[9]	274704	268172	44208	13.2	-3.6
Anxiety disorders[10]	42407	274615	26417	13.1	-0.7

Source: GBD 2016 Disease and Injury Incidence and Prevalence Collaborators (2017)

The following subsections provide detail evidence based on WHO data.

Disease Burden Estimates

Global disease burden of mental disorders is estimated to account for 30% of non-fatal disease burden worldwide and 10% of overall disease burden, including death and disability as per WHO estimates in 2012. In a 2018 Global Burden of Disease (GBD) study of 195 countries, covering the time span from 1990 to 2017, the authors report that mental disorders have consistently formed more than 14% of age-standardized YLDs for nearly three decades, and have greater than 10% prevalence in all 21 GBD regions (GBD 2017 Disease and Injury Incidence and Prevalence Collaborators, Lancet 2018). In a re-estimation of published data and adjusting for underestimation of the global burden, Vigo, Thornicroft, and Atun (2016) have upgraded the previous estimates for 2013, showing that the global burden of mental illness accounted for 32.4% of YLDs and 13.0% of DALYs, instead of the earlier estimates suggesting 21.2% of YLDs and 7.1% of DALYs. The burden of mental and substance use disorders around the globe is, now, largely driven by population growth and aging[11]; which means the burden is more likely to maintain an upward trend.

As evident from the following Table 2, mental and substance abuse disorders, within the group of NCDs, ranked as leading cause of YLDs (Table 2 below and Whiteford et al. 2013, 2015).

Table 2. The Contribution Major Non-communicable dis- eases YLD as a proportion of global disease burden (from all causes) (2000 and 2016)

Global Disease Burden	2000	2016
Non-communicable Diseases	77	79
Mental and Substance Use Disorders	21-23	21
Sense Organ Diseases	13	13
Musculoskeletal	12	13
Neurological Conditions	7	7
Injuries	7	7

Source: WHO, Global Burden of Disease Databases and GBD 2016 Disease and Injury Incidence and Prevalence Collaborators, Lancet 2017

As per the estimates of Vigo et al (2016), five types of mental illness appeared in the top 20 causes of global burden of disease (GBD) in 2013: major depression (2nd rank), anxiety disorders (7th rank), Schizophrenia (11th rank), Dysthymia (16th rank) and Bipolar disorder (17th rank). Most frequently occurring disorders are known as "common" mental disorders referring to two main diagnostic categories: depressive disorders and anxiety disorders. Of the total YLDs attributable to M&SUD, these common disorders contributed 47 percent depressive disorders accounting for above 29% (GBD 2016 Disease and Injury Incidence and Prevalence Collaborators, Lancet 2017). Data from 1990 to 2017 reveals that depressive disorders ranked 3rd in 2017 as one of the leading causes of disability, shifting up from its 4th place in 1990 (Institute for Health Metrics and Evaluation IHME, 2018). Evidence confirms depression to be the single largest contributor to global dis- ability (7.5% of all YLDs in 2015); anxiety disorders ranked 6th (3.4%) (WHO 2017c). In the following Table 3, it is observed that depressive disorders have the highest YLD counts compared to other mental and substance use disorders. Depression disorder has relatively high lifetime prevalence ranging from 2% to 15% and is associated with substantial disability (Moussavi et al 2007).

The changes in the disease burden are generally reported through two summary measures: the mean percentage change in number of YLDs and the mean percentage change in age-standardized YLD rates. The mean percentage change in the number of YLDs reflects the combined effects of population growth, population ageing, and epidemiological change. The mean percent change in age-standardized YLD rate, on the other hand, reflects epidemiological change that is not due to ageing or population growth (GBD 2016 Disease and Injury Incidence and Prevalence Collaborators, 2017). Compared to the age-standardized rates, the absolute number of YLDs from mental and substance use has been growing rapidly across all socio-demographic index quintiles, partly because of population growth, but also due to the ageing of populations. Demographic changes (with an increased proportion of the population reaching a higher age) have increased the time individuals are at risk for a number of late-onset diseases. The longer lifespan (mean number of years lived by the corresponding population) of individuals living in high-income countries, is an increasing challenge for the mental illness and the disability burden.[12] Globally, the population is ageing rapidly. Between 2015 and 2050, the proportion of the world's population more than 60 years old will nearly double, from 12% to 22% (WHO 2017).

Table 3. Disease Burden and Changes over 2007-2017: YLD Counts and Age Standardized Rates

Over all and disease Specific YLDs	YLDs ('000) Counts	Percentage change in Counts (YLDs) 2007-2017	Percentage change in age-standardized (YLDs) rates, 2007–17
All Causes YLDs 2017	853042.6	29.8	-0.9
Non- Communicable YLDs 2017	678294.4	19.3	0.1
Mental Disorders YLDs 2017	122746.3	13.5	-1.1
Depressive Disorders, YLD 2017	43099.9	14.3	-2.6
Anxiety Disorders, YLD 2017	27 121.4	12.8	-1.2
Schizophrenia, YLD 2017	12657.9	17.2	-0.3
Bipolar disorder YLD 2017	9293.8	15.2	1.2
Substance Use Disorders 2017	31052.9	16.7	2.9

Source: GBD 2017 Disease and Injury Incidence and Prevalence Collaborators (2018)

Comorbidity[13]

Mental disorders often affect, and are affected by, other diseases such as cancer, cardiovascular disease and HIV infection/Acquired Immunodeficiency Syndrome (AIDS) (WHO 2013). Epidemiological surveys have consistently endorsed the occurrence of comorbid psychiatric and substance use disorders among adults. Comorbidity has been found to be the norm for both mental and physical disorders (Gadermann, Alonso, Vilagut, Zaslavsky & Kessler 2012). In persons over the age of 60, the simultaneous presence of two or more diseases (comorbidity) has become the rule rather than an exception (Sartorious 2013). The growing burden of comorbidity, which increases with age, has been confirmed by the 2013 GBD study covering the period from 1990 to 2013 (Lancet 2015).

Though mental health conditions are a considerable disease burden across the globe, there is evidence of regional variations in the prevalence of common mental disorders. Even within a country, there is consistent evidence of regional variations in prevalence rates (Lewis and Booth 1992, Reijneveld, & Schene 1998). The 2010 GBD study estimates show that mental disorder DALYs are highest in the Middle East and North African regions, SUD DALYs are highest in Eastern Europe and Central Asian regions, and neurological disorder DALYs are highest in South Asia (Whiteford et al 2015). Variations across global regions can be due to myriad factors, such as national policies, plans and laws for mental health, human and financial resources available, socioeconomic development level, as well as violations of international human rights (e.g., equality, justice and human dignity) standards at country/ regional level. Since childhood and adolescence is a highly sensitive period of emotional and mental health, national policies that do not shield children and young people from adversity and social abuses can be a considerable risk factor for mental disorders.

As per the study by Steel et al (2014), regional evidence for North and Southeast Asia in particular has consistently shown lower one-year and lifetime prevalence estimates than other regions (Steel et al 2014). One-year prevalence rates have also been found to be lower in Sub-Saharan-Africa. Table 4 below presents the estimates of the burden of leading major disorders-depressive and anxiety disorders across the WHO regions It is observed that YLD rates from depressive disorders vary across WHO Regions, from 640 YLDs per 100 000 people in the Western Pacific Region to over 850 YLDs in low-and middle-income countries (LMICs) of the European Region (WHO

2017). YLDs from anxiety disorders varied from 267 YLDs per 100 000 people in the African Region to over 500 YLDs in the Region of the Americas. Disease burden estimates are lower for anxiety disorders compared to depression because these disorders are associated with a lower average level of disability (WHO 2017).

Table 4. Global and Regional Estimates of YLDs from Common Mental Disorders: 2015

WHO Regions	Depressive Disorders YLDs per 100,000	Anxiety Disorders YLDs per 100,000
AFR	731	267
EMR	685	354
EUR	859	302
Americas	844	567
SEAR	724	286
WPR	640	274
World	738	335

Source: WHO 2017

Age-Specific DALYs

Prevalence of psychiatric disorders is sensitive to specific age groups. To facilitate international comparisons, the YLD estimates of mental disorders across countries/regions require techniques that adjust for variations in the age structure of populations. An age-adjusted rate is a measure that controls for the effects of age differences on health event rates. Crude rates, on the other hand, provide a useful summary measure to compare similar populations of different sizes. But crude rates are sensitive to differences in age compositions. Differences in age can distort other comparisons between populations, and this distortion is called confounding. Adjusted rates are generally preferred because they allow for comparison of populations with different demographic structures. However, the main criticism levelled at age-standardized rates is the requirement of selecting an arbitrary standard population as a representative population for countries in comparison. It is suggested that age-standardized rates can be meaningfully compared only if they refer to the same standard (Bray and Ferlay 2019).

The results from the two methods (crude rates and standardized), as shown in Table 3, present a diverging picture of the changes in mental disorders over time. Despite mostly stagnant age-standardized rates, the absolute number of YLDs from NCDs has been growing over time, partly because of population growth, but also the ageing of populations. To remedy the comparability issue across world regions, age-specific rates can be computed using the WHO database. The following Tables 5 and 6 present age-specific rates of DALYs per thousands of people for each age group across world regions for 2000 and 2016.

Table 5. Burden of mental and substance use disorders: 2000

Table 5	DALYs per 000 people 2000						
	5-14 years	15-29 years	30-49 years	50-59 years	60-69 years	70+ years
M&SUD DALY Per head ('000)						
Global	10.5	27.8	32.6	30.9	28.3	22.9
Europe	11.00	34.9	42.8	37.7	31.1	23.0
Americas	10.5	36.1	41.7	35.1	28.5	21.1
SEARS	10.2	23.8	28.8	28.6	27.3	23.7
EMR	11.6	29.8	33.7	28.5	25.7	22.00
WPR	9.7	24.2	26.9	27.1	27.2	23.0
Africa	11.8	27.4	30.3	29.6	28.6	27.1

Source: Data Compiled from WHO Disease Burden Databases

Table 6. Burden of mental and substance use disorders: 2016

Table 6	5-14 years	15-29 years	30-49 years	50-59 years	60-69 years	70+ years
\multicolumn{7}{c}{DALYs per 000 people 2016}						
\multicolumn{7}{c}{M&SUD DALY Per head ('000)}						
Global	10.3	27.3	30.9	29.2	27.3	22.2
Europe	10.6	32.8	38.4	34.0	29.5	21.8
Americas	11.0	37.1	40.3	35.5	27.8	20.1
SEARS	10.1	22.9	27.7	27.0	26.2	23.0
EMR	11.2	29.8	33.5	28.4	25.6	21.4
WPR	8.8	23.6	26.0	26.0	26.9	22.9
Africa	11.2	27.3	29.3	28.2	27.6	26.2

Source: Data Compiled from WHO Disease Burden Databases

The breakdown of YLDs by age groups of the population in these tables shows a high concentration of disability burden among adolescents and adults (aged 15–29 and 30–49).[14] This age group represents more than 54% of the global population. Patel et al. (2010) estimated that at any given time, approximately 10% of children and adults suffer from one or more mental disorders. According to a 2014 WHO study, one in four or five young people (aged 12–24) is estimated to suffer from a mental disorder in any one year, notwithstanding substantial variations in prevalence between regions (WHO 2014). Data on YLD in Tables 5 and 6 suggests that the mental burden has remained almost stagnant for each age group over one and half decades.

2.2.1 DISEASE BURDEN AMONG CHILDREN AND YOUNG ADULTS

Mental illnesses are quite prevalent among children and youth.

Epidemiological facts confirm that about half of all mental illnesses appear before the age of 14, and 75% develop by age 24 (Kessler et al. 2007). Young people aged 10-24 represent 27% of the world's population at present (Gore et al. 2011). The GBD project and country-wide epidemiological surveys similarly reveal that many mental illnesses—between 50% and about 70%—show up before the age of 18, so they can have a huge impact on a child's development (Whiteford et al. 2013; WHO 2014). In their global study of young people (aged 10-24 years), Gore et al (2011) found evidence of neuropsychiatric disorders (including substance use) being the main cause of YLDs in all the regions of the world. In high income countries, these authors also found neuropsychiatric disorders to be the main cause of DALYs, especially in those aged 15-24 years. In United States, approximately one in every four or five youth meets criteria for a mental disorder with severe impairment in their lifetime (Merikangas et al 2010). Even in the category of chronic mental afflictions, the National Alliance of Mental Illness (NAMI) has noted that one-half of all chronic mental illness begins by the age of 14, three-quarters by age 24. The following subsection provides a brief sketch about childhood behavioral disorders, which as a category is now the sixth leading cause of disease burden among adolescents (WHO, Fact sheets, Adolescents Mental Health).

The contexts and environment that children live in today have been rapidly changing and can have a considerable impact on their well-being. Over the last two decades, family structure has changed on several fronts, with increasing rates of divorce, children born outside of marriage, and single parent households. The share of divorced or separated parents has increased across many OECD countries since the mid-1990s, with an average of around 10% in the latest available year with data (OECD 2018). Risks of cyberbullying contact with strangers, sexual messaging ('sexting') and pornography generally affect one in five adolescents (Livingstone and Smith (2014). Teenagers access social media sites from cell phones, and as reviewed in a recent clinical report from the American Academy of Pediatrics, social media, mainly Facebook, offers opportunities and potential risks to young wired users (American Academy of Pediatrics Policy statement 2013).

Children all over the world face numerous other risk factors and challenges, including extreme poverty, childhood adversity, family violence, neglect, child abuse, street life, and child labor practices (Polanczky 2013). Most striking to note is that 91% of the world's children live in LMICs, where these risk factors make their childhood years highly vulnerable to mental and physical sickness (Erskine et al. 2015). YLD rates have remained constant or possibly increased due to mental disorders in this age group (see also Baranne and Falissard 2018).

Analyzing the risk factors faced by youth populations in the early adulthood age group (aged 20–24), a 2014 WHO report mentions various risk factors such as the risk of unemployment, poor quality employment (such as employment with no or short-term contracts, and jobs with low reward and control at work), debt burden, and relative socioeconomic status have significant harmful impacts on mental health. This age group is also the one where YLDs, due to substance abuse, is much higher than in other age groups. The economic and social status of youth can have widespread effects that influence children, partners, and the greater family, communities, economic development, and sub- sequent generations (WHO 2014a). Those youth who are homeless and street-involved, orphaned, victims of violence, and those involved with the juvenile justice and mental-health systems face increased likelihood of mental health impairment and disability (UN 2014). Mental disorders in adolescence often carry into adulthood (Aneshensel and Sucoff 1996).

Longitudinal studies[15] have found that occurrence of mental and substance disorders at a young age runs the risk of chronic and recurrent mental disorders and disabling conditions in adulthood (Erskine et al. 2015). Mental disorders among youth and the associated functional impairment have far-reaching consequences, not only for those affected but also for their families and their social- and work-related environments (Trautmann, Rehm, and Wittchen 2016). Mental and sub- stance-use disorders among youth and adolescents are associated with negative social, educational, and economic outcomes, with financial costs to health and other services such as the criminal justice system.

The following section reviews the social and economic impact associated with the mental illness.

2.3 SOCIAL AND ECONOMIC IMPACT OF MENTAL DISORDERS

The economic impact of mental disorders is wide ranging, long lasting, and enormous. Whiteford et al. (2015) noted that mental and substance-abuse disorders increased a person's risk of other diseases and injuries, including suicide. Another alarming research finding is that DALYs from mental and substance use peak in early adulthood, a time of life when individuals start to make a significant social and economic contribution to families and societies (White, Ford et al. 2015).

Several studies have documented that most of the costs associated with mental health problems extend beyond the health care sector (Ngui et al. 2010). These costs take the form of reduced productivity in the workplace (Goetze et al. 2003), absenteeism, sick leave, early retirement, and receipt of disability pensions. The direct (medical expenditure) and indirect cost (in the form of broader societal impact like reduced productivity) of mentally ill health can exceed 4% of GDP (OECD 2014a).

At the household level, evidence shows that the costs directly associated with mental illness take the form of reduced earnings and additional (and sometimes "catastrophic") out-of-pocket expenditures on health care services. These expenditures often lead to a decrease in household spending, selling of household assets, and depletion of savings (WHO 2013b). Individuals with mental illness are likely to be poor, stigmatized, and socially excluded. They often become victims of human rights violations, both within and outside of psychiatric institutions (WHO 2013b), which in turn, severely restricts their capabilities for reproduction, education, standards of health, and work (Ngui et al. 2010; WHO 2013a). Serious mental illness causes critical functional impairment that substantially interferes with or limits one or more major life activities (National Institute of Mental Health, Information Page). Mental-health conditions affect youths' self-esteem, social interactions, and can even increase their chances of personal injury and harming themselves and others (UN 2014).

The comorbidity of mental disorders with other disorders like substance abuse and physical debility can have adverse consequences such as poverty, marginalization, and social disadvantage (Lancet 2007; WHO 2010a). The disease burden from M&SUD is known to exceed HIV and cancer in terms of numbers of individuals affected (Üstün 1999). According to the OECD (2014a), approximately one-third of new disability benefit claims in 2008 were attributable to mental disorders. This figure was as high as 50% in some rural areas. Furthermore, as noted in the aforementioned OECD study, virtually all OECD countries experienced a large increase in these claims from 1987 to 2008. "Intangible" costs, such as the emotional distress, pain, and suffering experienced by those with an enduring mental illness (OECD 2014a) can result in concurrent disorder (substance use) and physical comorbidity conditions. Studies have adduced evidence of treatment gaps for serious mental disorders in every country, which expose them to higher risks of role disability (inability to carry out usual activities) and greater adverse effects on role function with many serious chronic physical illnesses (WHO 2001).

Additionally, there is clear evidence of mental disorders accounting for a large proportion of the disease burden in young people even in high-in- come countries (Patel et al. 2007). The NAMI (2013) reports that approximately 20% of youth ages 13 to 18 experience severe mental disorders in a given year. For ages 8 to 15, the rate is 13%. It is estimated that for U.S. students, over 50% of students with a mental health condition, who are age 14 and older and served by special education will drop out, which translates to the highest dropout rate of any disability group.

Evidence indicates that most mental health needs in young people are unmet (Patel et al. 2007). Young and adolescent people need timely intervention for redressing mental health issues before they become involved in the juvenile justice system (Kutcher and McDougall 2009). Disorders such as schizophrenia have been found to be associated with increased risk of crime among both men and women regardless of socio- economic status or marital status (Brennan, Mednick, and Hodgins 2000; Walsh, Buchanan, and Fahy 2002). The studies by Tiihonen and colleagues (1997) and Fazel and colleagues (2009) similarly reported a higher risk for violent behavior associated with alcohol-induced psychoses, with schizophrenia, and coexisting with substance abuse.

3. SOCIOECONOMIC DETERMINANTS OF MENTAL HEALTH (CSDH FRAMEWORK)

Health disparities exist within every country and across nations. To explain the determinants of population health, WHO developed a conceptual framework of social determinants of health, known as the Commission on Social Determinants of Health (CSDH) (Solar 2010). This CSDH model is briefly described in Figure 1. This framework defines social determinants of health as "the conditions in which people are born, grow, live, work and age." These conditions are "shaped by the distribution of money, power, and resources at global, national, and local levels." Social determinants operate at two main levels: structural and proximal (Viner et al. 2012; WHO 2008). Structural mechanisms are rooted in the key institutions and policies of the socioeconomic and political context. Proximal determinants are shaped in part by stratifications resulting from the structural determinants. These determinants are represented by socioeconomic indicators such as income, education, occupation, social class, gender, and race/ ethnicity that determine access to resources, including educational opportunities (Solar 2010). The structural determinants work through a series of intermediary (proximal) social factors or social determinants of health. The proximal factors include social surroundings such as family (e.g., quality of the family environment), school (such as school, peer relationships, social skills development programs), and neighborhood environmental factors. Studies have also labeled structural determinants as "upstream factors." These upstream factors influence mental health through shaping social determinants located "downstream" (i.e., near where health effects are observed, see Braveman and Gottlieb 2014; Crompton and Shim 2015; Phelon et al. 2010; Viner et al. 2012; WHO 2014; Wilkinson and Marmot 2013; Williams et al. 2008). Upstream social determinants of health play a more fundamental causal role in creating health disparities. Understanding the causal mechanism is important from the viewpoint of mitigating health inequalities.

Figure 1. Social Determinants of Health (WHO Framework)

SOCIOECONOMIC AND POLITICAL CONTEXT			
Governance	Social Hierarchy — Social Structure, Social Class	Socioeconomic Position	SOCIAL DETERMINANTS OF HEALTH → IMPACT ON EQUITY IN HEALTH AND WELL-BEING
Macroeconomic Policies — Labour Market Structure	Class: has an economic base and access resources	Social Class, Gender, Ethnicity	(INTERMEDIARY FACTORS)
Social Policies — Labour Market, Housing, Land	Power is related to a political context	Education	
Public Policies — Health, Education, Social Protection	Prestige or honour in the community	Occupation	
Culture and Societal Values	Discrimination	Income	

STRUCTURAL DETERMINANTS
SOCIAL DETERMINNANTS OF HEALTH INEQUITIES

Source: Solar and Irwin (2010). A conceptual framework for action on the social determinants of health. Social Determinants of Health Discussion Paper 2 (Policy and Practice). WHO.

3.1 SOCIAL DETERMINANTS OF MENTAL HEALTH INEQUITIES: CAUSATION VERSUS SELECTION HYPOTHESIS

Research into the relationship between lower socioeconomic status and mental health tends to posit two hypotheses: social causation and social selection (or drift). Social causation suggests that poverty may lead to "mental disorders" through pathways of stress or deprivation or decreasing the likelihood of people getting treatment. Conversely, social selection "posits that genetically predisposed persons drift down to or fail to rise out of poverty," meaning that downward mobility is linked to "family liability to mental illness" (Costello et al. 2003;

Dohrenwend et al. 1992). To study incidences, causes, and prognoses, cohort studies are used as they measure events in chronological order to distinguish between cause and effect (Mann 2003).

Lorant et al. (2003), in their study linking socioeconomic status (SES) and mental depression, supported the contention that causation (low SES increases risk of depression) had the edge over selection (depression hinders social mobility), although both processes were at play. Patel et al. (2018), in their systematic review of 26 studies from mostly high-income countries, found that nearly two-thirds of all studies and five out of six longitudinal studies reported a statistically significant positive relationship between income inequality and risk of depression. Moreover, Hudson's 2005 longitudinal study revealed a remarkably strong and consistent negative correlation between socioeconomic conditions (based on community income, education, and employment status) and mental illness. In fact, a number of studies noted that the relationship between poor economic status and ill health reflected causality running in both directions: poverty bred ill-health, and ill-health kept poor people poor (Dohrenwend et al. 1992; Saxena et al. 2007; Wagstaff 2002). Among affected families, financial hardships are further aggravated primarily due to reduced earnings from "sickness absence," underperformance, and workplace disability.

3.2 SELECTION OF PREDICTORS OF MENTAL HEALTH

The growing burden of mental health warrants remedial actions. Data show that there are ample variations in the prevalence of mental disorders across OECD countries. An attempt is made in the present study to identify factors that account for most variations in these developed nations. On the basis of the CSDH framework and evidence available from existing studies, the present empirical study selected the following structural determinants of mental illness (see Table 7): income disparities and poverty, the prevalence of precarious (nonstandard) employment, the percentage of children with single-parent households, housing affordability, and the extent of wealth inequalities.

Table 7. Selected Structural Determinants

Structural Determinants and Indicator of Measurement
Wealth Inequality-Gini Coefficient
Income Inequality-Income Quintile ratio
Precarious Employment -Employment Protection Legislation (EPL)
Economic Conditions of Youth – Youth (15-25 age group poverty rate (relative threshold, OECD)
Housing Cost Burden – median rent paid by bottom quintile as percent of their disposable income
Family Factors(Demographic)- Percentage of Children with Single Parent Household

Sources: OECD (databases); Credit Suisse Wealth Report.

In addition to these structural determinants, the role of the health care system and its resources on the prevalence of disorders across countries was examined. The mental health care system of a country, though a nonsocial determinant, is integral to human health and well-being of a nation (WHO 2014a). Through the provision of fundamental services in a community and primary health care setting, a country's mental health system can be designed to fulfill the objective of recovery-oriented mental care (Anthony 1993). Each of these determinants of mental illness are explained in the paragraphs below.

3.2.1 INCOME INEQUALITY

Income inequality and the poverty that goes with it are among the leading causes of health issues (Murali and Oyebode 2004; Raphael 2002). Research into poverty and inequality often concentrates on income as a measure of economic well-being, usually by classifying households as poor that have an income below a certain proportion of the mean or median household income. Gold et al. (2002) studied the health of the teenage population in the United States and found that while poverty had a direct effect on mental health status, income inequality exerted its effects principally through social capital[16]-social cohesion, civic engagement, and mutual trust in a community. Viner et al. (2012) found income inequality among the strongest structural factors influencing mental health (in addition to national wealth and access to education). Studies have distinguished two alternative pathways through which income inequalities affect mental health status specifically (Lynch and Kaplan 2000, Macinko et al 2003). These include psychosocial pathways and neo-material pathways.

Psychosocial pathways and neo-material pathways: Two Alternative Pathways of Inequality and Mental Health Relationship

As per the psychosocial hypothesis of "status anxiety," individuals are assumed to compete for status and prestige in social hierarchies, and being unsuccessful in this status competition (that is, receiving negative appraisals of one's status) leads to stress (Marmot 2004; Wilkinson and Pickett 2010). Wilkinson and Picket (2009b), in their book The Spirit Level, have argued that inequality creates greater social competition and divisions, which in turn fosters increased social anxiety and higher stress and thus greater incidence of mental illness, dissatisfaction, and resentment. Psychosocial variables are generally proxied by the indicators: perception of control over life, anxiety, insecurity, depression, the degree of racism, discrimination, and low social cohesion in social affiliations, existence of socially hazardous environments, and bullying; all of which affect mental health through neuroendocrine pathways (Marmot and Wilkinson 2001). In a meta-analysis of 208 studies by Dickerson and Kemeny (2004), the researchers found that stress-hormone (cortisol) levels were raised particularly by "social evaluative threats" (that is, when people felt that others were making negative judgments about them (Rowlingson 2011).

Relative inequality with respect to income translates into absolute inequality with respect to capabilities (Sen 1992). Relative deprivation[17] relates to a broader approach to social functioning and the meeting of human needs or "capabilities," in the words of Sen (Marmot 2005, p. 1102). In other words, income inequality for individuals implies deprivation across multiple domains including health, education, employment, housing, and participating in society (WHO 2014a)

Lynch and Kaplan (2000), on the other hand, reject the role of relative status, instead stressing the prominence of the distribution of a country's resources. In their view, countries with high inequality tended to invest less in public goods, such as infrastructure, technology, and education. Based on this neo-materialistic perspective, the economically poor segment of the population with inadequate health coverage remained undertreated/untreated due to a lack of resources and access to timely care.

In the real world, however, it is difficult to isolate the effects of psychosocial factors and neo-material factors on health (McLeod et al. 2003; Patel et al. 2018; Pearce and Smith 2003; Van de Werfhorst and Salverda 2012) since socioeconomic structure has a powerful psychosocial as well as material effect (Marmot and Wilkinson 2001). In a study by Van Oort, van Len, and Mackenbach (2005), neo-material factors were assumed to affect mortality either directly or indirectly, via behavioral and psychosocial factors.

3.2.2 WEALTH INEQUALITY

Family wealth is considered a strong predictor of peoples' mental health. Wealth inequality as a causal factor may be less prone to health selection bias (i.e., reverse causation) than income because it is less immediately sensitive to short-term changes in earning capacity (Carter et al. 2009; Lê-Scherban, Brenner, and Schoeni 2016). Wealth (or net worth) is a measure of accumulated economic resources, often over a lifetime that is therefore less influenced by recent economic shocks. Carter et al. (2009) found, based on their study of the New Zealand economy, that the strength of the association of wealth with psychological distress was stronger than it was that of income. They found that inequalities in wealth were strongly associated with psychological distress, over and above other confounding demographic variables and baseline health status. In their view, individuals who had financial or physical assets could feel more in control of their lives, resulting in less vulnerability to anxiety or mood disorders, or to severe psychological symptoms. Wealth is a marker for social status and respectability, just as poverty is a marker for stigmatization (Marmot and Wilkinson 2001). The flipside of wealth is debt (OECD 2015a).

Corporate market power is deemed to be a powerful mechanism of transferring wealth from the many among the working and middle classes to the few belonging to the 1% and 0.1% at the top of the income and wealth distribution. Estimating the impact of market power on wealth inequality, Ennis, Gonzaga, and Pike (2017) found that, on average, excessive market power accounted for between 6% and 21% of the wealth of the top decile in OECD countries. Khan and Vaheesan (2017) contend that monopoly pricing on goods and services turn the disposable income of the many into capital gains, dividends, and executive compensation for the few. Although there is no satisfactory metric that can measure corporate power, the power of corporations can be assessed by looking at the strength of countervailing forces seeking to limit the influence of corporations—that is, the strength of the trade unions.

3.2.3 EMPLOYMENT STATUS AND YOUTH POVERTY

Employment status and working conditions are among the most prominent structural determinants of an individual's socioeconomic position within a society (Benach, Muntaner, and Santana 2007b; Lynch and Kaplan 2000; Wilkinson and Marmot 2003; WHO 2007b). Work and working conditions are essential contributors to social inequality in health within and across generations (Burgard and Lin 2013). These conditions refer to terms of employment, like contractual stability of employment, rewards, and other mutual expectations between workers and employers (Benach et al. 2014).

Since the mid-1970s, standard employment across a few sectors has shifted to nonstandard forms of employment (NSE or precarious employment), including temporary work, part-time work, temporary agency work and subcontracting, dependent self-employment, and disguised employment relationships (ILO 2016). Globally, more than half of all jobs created since 1995 are nonstandard jobs (Förster 2015), and a large majority of these workers (at least 80%) live in households consisting of two or more people, which often include children (OECD 2015). The emerging research describes precarious employment as a social determinant of health and emphasizes that poor-quality patterns of employment both reflect and reinforce the social gradient (Benach et al. 2014; Marmot and Bell 2012b). Benach et al. (2010) defined the number of working poor as a component of precarious employment and used this as a proxy for employment instability and unsustainability.

The new nonstandard form of employment are associated with lower wages, fewer opportunities for training, limited access to social protection, and other work-related benefits. An increase in part-time, insecure, and low-paid employment widens the gap between rich and poor and are key predictors of the decline in social cohesion among other factors (Kawachi & Kennedy 1997, Chuang, Chuang, and Yang 2013). Empirical evidence indicates that employment is robustly associated with reduced symptoms of depression and anxiety as well as decreased suicide prevalence, especially among men (Lund et al. 2018). Employment acts as an important protective factor against mental disorders and is associated with better social functioning, less severe symptoms, higher quality of life, and improved self-esteem in people living with schizophrenia and bipolar disorder (Lund et al. 2018).

Youth poverty and mental health

According to the International Labour Organization report (2017), youth are three times as likely as adults to be unemployed and twice as likely as adults to be in temporary employment. This report also explains that globally, three out of four employed young women and men are in informal employment, compared to three in five for adults. In 2015, the share of young workers in the EU-28 categorized as being at risk of poverty (measured as earning less than 60% of the median income) was 12.5%, compared to 9.5% among prime-age workers (25–54 years old; ILO 2017, p. 33).

Among the working poor, younger workers—especially those with temporary contracts—face lower prospects of moving on to more stable employment with opportunities for upward mobility (OECD 2015). Job market challenges have made it more difficult for young adults to attain the economic stability and self-sufficiency that are important markers of the transition to adulthood (Danziger Ratner 2010). Youth across developed economies face much of the burden of insecure jobs and are at greater risk of spending their lives in poverty, as compared with the elderly (Aassve et al. 2005; OECD 2011). The inherent uncertainty of securing the next work assignment can heighten job-related stress among young people (ILO 2017). Low-wage, part-time positions, precarious work, and poverty limit housing options as well as reduce the ability to form relationships and hinder the ability to start a family (OECD 2011). It is estimated that in OECD countries, 18% of the youth population live below 60% of the median income. Poverty and social disadvantage strongly associate with high levels of stress and mental disorders (Patel et al. 2007). Anxiety and depressive disorders are about twice as common in low-income and low-education groups relative to high-income and high-education groups (Alegria et al. 2000; Wang 2000). A longitudinal study (Benjet et al. 2012) of Mexican youth found that jobs available to young people without post-secondary education or experience were likely to put them in high risk situations, compromise their well-being, and hinder their professional development. Analysis of a large data set from 26 European Union countries from 1970 to 2007 showed that every 1% increase in unemployment was associated with a 0.79% rise in suicides at ages younger than 65 years (WHO 2014a). The findings from longitudinal studies and country studies by WHO (2014a) show three important relations: (i) high associations between unemployment and an increased risk of depression, (ii) the strong link of job insecurity with suboptimal mental health, and (iii) the protective effect of strong social welfare systems against unemployment risks for mental disorders.

It is feared that young people with mental illnesses may become vulnerable to stigma and social isolation, and failure to address their mental health needs might cause further alienation and lead to crime and other forms of social unrest. Falling participation rates and a net loss of employment for young people are reflected in rising numbers of youth not employed or enrolled in education or training programs (NEET) in many OECD countries (Carcillo et al. 2015). Estimates indicate that this number is as high as 21.8% of young people.

Causal link between precarious employment and mental health: empirical evidence

The association between nonstandard/precarious employment and mental health has been explored and documented in several empirical studies (de Graaf et al. 2002; Dooley, Prause, and Ham-Rowbottom 2000; Moscone, Tosetti, and Vittadini 2016; OECD Employment Outlook 2008; Vives et al. 2013). Demonstrating a link between socioeconomic background (such as income or occupation) and health, the well-known Whitehall II study, which followed more than 10,000 UK civil servants since 1985, found that stress levels were amplified as workers descended the organizational hierarchy—with corresponding declines in health. Workers on the bottom of the heap were far more likely to suffer coronary heart disease than those at the top (Rowlingson 2011). A review of 15 studies found the median ratio between the one-year prevalence of mental disorders among individuals in the lowest socioeconomic category and the prevalence of mental disorders among individuals in the highest socioeconomic category was 2.1:1. The median ratio for lifetime prevalence among individuals in those same socioeconomic categories was 1.4:1 (Kohn et al. 1998). Similar results have been reported from various studies carried out in North America, Latin America, and Europe (WHO International Consortium of Psychiatric Epidemiology 2000; WHO 2001, p. 40). Studies have now conjectured that causation and selection are, in fact, not mutually exclusive explanations and that they may be combined over the life cycle (Lorant et al. 2003). Evidence for selection hypothesis suggests that mental health status also affects future employment opportunities (de Lange et al. 2005; Olesen et al. 2013). Abundant evidence confirms that mental disorders increase the likelihood of living in poverty, perhaps because of the influence on functionality and the ability to secure or sustain employment. There is a strong relationship between poor mental health and social deprivation, with causal influences acting bi-directionally (OECD Employment Outlook 2015; Social Exclusion Unit 2004).

Poor employment quality and mental health risk

Poor employment status and low earnings may influence the worker's mental health through multiple channels: (a) unmet mental health needs arising from high out-of-pocket expenses and the lack of employer-paid benefits (health insurance coverage, sick leave benefits), (b) mental stress due to status anxiety, perceived job uncertainty, and lack of career growth prospects, and (c) work-life conflict. The details are given below.

Unmet Mental Health Needs: In today's employment environment, even paid employment can leave workers and families in financial poverty for two basic reasons: (a) insufficient productive employment opportunities and (b) inadequate pay rates (Wicks-Lim 2012). Low- wage jobs contribute to generating a class of working poor (Wicks-Lim 2012). At today's low wage level, hourly workers more often face underwork than overwork, as well as fluctuating, unstable schedules. Part-time workers face difficulty in saving for retirement, planning for the future, and overall, they earn less money than needed. Workers employed under NSE contracts frequently have inadequate employment-based social security coverage, either because they are explicitly excluded from receiving coverage by law or because their short tenure, short contribution periods, or low earnings may limit access to such entitlements (ILO 2015c). Temporary and part-time workers are much less likely to receive health insurance and retirement benefits, or other "fringe benefits," in addition to being paid less (Kalleberg 2006). Lack of social protection may create another leap toward deprivation and associated health consequences (Benach et al. 2016).

Perceived Job Insecurity and Mental Disorders: In precarious employment, workers have no protection of rights through a collective bargaining process and no regulatory protection through union representation or the law (Cranford, Vosko, and Zukewich 2003). To explore a causal link of job insecurity and mental health, studies have emphasized the distinction between job loss and job insecurity (Burgard, Brand, and House 2009; Ferrie et al. 2008; Vives et al. 2013). It is contended that the job loss is immediate (in that, it relieves at least one major source of stress—that of uncertainty), whereas job insecurity is an everyday experience involving prolonged uncertainty about the future (Sverke, Hellgren, and Näswall 2002). In these authors' view, "given that job insecurity reflects a worry about losing the present job, this subjective experience is likely to have a strong psychological impact" (p. 2). Burgard, Brand, and House (2009), based on their longitudinal study, obtained strong evidence for the (causal) link between perceived insecurity and mental health (depressive symptoms and negative feelings). The study by László et al. (2010), covering 16 European countries, found that persons with insecure jobs were at risk for poor health even in those European countries that had good welfare regimes. Job insecurity aggravates mental stress when unemployment is recurrent or persistent, when unemployment benefits are low relative to previous earnings, or when workers have to accept major cuts in pay, hours, or both to find a new job. Empirical evidence indicates that job insecurity reduces psychological well-being and job satisfaction and increases psychosomatic complaints and physical strains (De Witte 1999).

Work-Life Conflict and Mental Stress: Work-life balance is considered a valuable function that enhances a person's capability to attain a better quality of life and choose a life of value (Hobson 2013). Studies have acknowledged that the imbalance between work and family life may be a stronger risk factor than work stress for mental disorders (Wang et al. 2008). Work-life conflict has increased with the spread of nonstandard and inadequate employment. Evidence shows that with the spread of precarious employment, the number of two-earner households increased, and families had to increase the time they spend at work to keep up with their income needs (Kalleberg

2009). With the spread of involuntary part-time jobs, workers are facing high odds of balancing multiple jobs at multiple work sites in order to earn a living wage. These multiple challenges create uncertainty about worker ability to provide for basic household needs (Lewchuk et al. 2003). Job insecurity, both perceived and attributed, has "spillover" effects on families (Ferrie 2001). Because both work and family roles represent core components of adult identity, impediments to both work- and family-related identity formation and maintenance are likely to be stressful (Chandola et al. 2004).

Sen's "capabilities" approach offers a theoretical space for capturing the growing divide between the domains of work and non-work areas of family life (Hobson 2011, 2013). The term capability refers not simply to what people are able to do but to their freedom to lead the kind of lives they value—and the kind of lives they have reason to value. Capabilities and well-being are related to the socioeconomic gradient through social determinants (WHO 2014). The capability of individual workers to obtain reasonable terms and conditions of employment is rooted in their bargaining power with employers in the labor market (ILO 2011). Experience shows that without workplace empowerment exercised through trade unions and collective bargaining representation, legal provisions and regulations often do not materialize in practice (ILO 2011). Studies have noted that temporary workers had, among other stressful and psychosocial working conditions, less freedom to choose when to take personal leave, less information about their work environment, fewer rights at work, less job autonomy, and less control over their schedules than workers with permanent contracts (Benach and Muntaner 2007). In a study involving 2,700 workers, Frone (2000) demonstrated that work-to-family conflict and family-to-work conflict were related positively to clinically significant diagnoses of mood, anxiety, and substance-dependence disorders.

3.2.4 AFFORDABILITY OF HOUSING

Poverty and associated conditions of deprivation and homelessness are not only widespread in poor countries, but also affect a sizeable minority of rich countries (WHO 2001). Estimates by NAMI (2018) show that in the United States approximately 26% of homeless adults staying in shelters live with serious mental illness and an estimated 46% live with severe mental illness and/or substance-use disorders.

OECD's "Affordable Housing Database" shows that housing needs are frequently unmet. Today a significant number of people across OECD countries are homeless and too many households live in low-quality dwellings or face housing costs they can ill afford. According to the data collected from the OECD Questionnaire on Affordable and Social Housing (QuASH), it is observed that homeless individuals represent a significant number of people in many OECD and EU countries (OECD 2016). The number of homeless people sharing housing with friends and relatives, particularly younger people, increased in many cities of Europe, according to the above report. Country analysis of this OECD report indicates that increased unemployment since the global financial crisis in 2008 has cut into welfare benefits. Barriers to health services and social services were also mentioned as potential contributors to a rise in homelessness and poverty.

3.2.5 SINGLE-PARENT HOUSEHOLDS, POVERTY, AND MENTAL STRESS

It is estimated that in-work poverty affects 8% of the working-age population—mainly single parents—in OECD countries (OECD 2017). Over the past two decades, in-work poverty has intensified mostly for single parents and for one-income couples with children (OECD 2017). Single-parent households are three times as likely as dual-parent households to be poor. Lack of income has been identified as the single most important factor in accounting for the differences in children from various family forms (Kirby 2004). There are more single-headed households with and without children today than ever before. The share of working-age single-parent households increased in all OECD countries, from an average of 15% in the late 1980s to 20% in the mid-2000s. On average, the poverty rate for single parents (32%) is three times higher than for all families with children (Förster and d'Ercole 2005). Smaller households are less able to benefit from the savings associated with pooling resources and sharing expenditures.

McLanahan and Sandfeur (1994) found that children of single mothers were at a higher risk for dropping out of high school and early pregnancy compared with those from two-parent families. In a study of the health of children in single-parent families in New Zealand, Tobias et al. (2010) found that children of single mothers between 5 and 14 years old were twice as likely as other children to have poor emotional health (and behavior patterns) but were only slightly more likely, if at all, to have worse physical health. For homeless groups, stressful living conditions become even more aggravated with insufficient community and institutional support (Elliott and Krivo 1991).

In the above discussion, the focus was on highlighting the role of socioeconomic determinants of mental disorders. The mental health care system of a country, though a nonsocial determinant, is integral to human health and well-being of a nation (WHO 2014a), and its vital role cannot go unstressed. A country's mental health resources include policy and infrastructure within countries, mental health services, community resources, human resources, and funding (Saxena et al. 2007). The challenges of health care systems overall and their resources are reviewed in section five.

4. EMPIRICAL ESTIMATES OF THE SOCIO- ECONOMIC DETERMINATES OF MENTAL DISORDERS

THIS STUDY uses the partial least square regression (PLSR) technique to determine the role of socioeconomic determinants that result in mental disorders. In particular, univariate PLSR is employed, in which we have one dependent variable (Y, prevalence of mental disorders) and six explanatory variables (see Table 7). In the PLSR approach, when we regress the dependent Y variable with the explanatory variables X1,...,Xp, PLSR attempts to find new factors that will play the same role as the X's. These new factors are often called latent variables or components (Garthwaite 1994, Yeniay and Goktas 2002). Each component is a linear combination of X1,...,Xp, which may be viewed as weighted averages of predictors, where each predictor holds the residual information in an explanatory variable that is not contained in earlier components (Garthwaite 1994). PLSR uses both the variation of X and Y to construct new factors that will play the role of explanatory variables (Yeniay and Goktas 2002). The PLSR approach is briefly explained in the appendix to this chapter. The following subsection reports the variables of the model and the empirical estimates of predictors.

Mental Disorder as a Dependent Variable

Mental disorders can be expressed by the prevalence rate or in terms of the disease burden, which is a DALY metric. DALYs for a disease are the sum of the YLLs due to premature mortality in the population and the YLD for incident cases of the health condition. To arrive at DALY, first the prevalence data is combined with disability weights to estimate YLDs. YLLs due to premature mortality are estimated by multiplying deaths occurring because of a given disorder by the reference standard life expectancy at the age death occurred.

Prevalence is a measure of disease that allows for the determination of a person's likelihood of having a disease. A prevalence rate is the total number of cases of a disease existing in a population divided by the total population. Prevalence differs from incidence of the disease. Incidence is a measure of disease that allows the determination of a person's probability of being newly diagnosed with a disease during a given period. An incidence rate is the number of new cases of a disease divided by the number of persons at risk for the disease. In nutshell, prevalence looks at existing cases, while incidence looks at new cases. The present study uses age-standardized prevalence rate data. Age-standardized rates account for the differences in the age structure of the populations being compared. For empirical estimation, the study uses the PLSR approach, which is briefly introduced below.

Explanatory Variables:Socio-Economic Determinants

There is well documented research evidence that social determinants are likely "fundamental causes" of mental disorders because they embody access to important resources throughout the life course of individuals. Based upon the overwhelming evidence on the role of socio-economic conditions, the present empirical exercise has attempted to identify the relative significance of some major socio-economic factors influencing the burden of mental disorders. The explanatory variables (listed in Table 7) considered in the present exercise include: wealth inequality; income inequality; strictness of EPL (employment protection legislation, measured on a scale from 0 to 6, with higher scores representing stricter regulation); youth (age group 15-25) poverty (relative threshold); housing cost burden (indicated by median rent paid by bottom quintile as a percentage of their disposable income); and percentage of children with a single parent household. The rationale for considering these factors as predictor variables has been explained in detail in section 3.2. As mentioned earlier, these explanatory variables constitute structural determinants of mental health.

Empirical Results

Before discussing the results, certain data limitations need to be mentioned. It is widely agreed that mental health problems and substance use disorders are still significantly underreported. This is true across all countries. Most common mental and neurological disorders in older adults co-occur with physical health conditions such as heart disease, and as such, may not be the result of the impact of social determinants alone. In addition, the state of a country's health system, its pattern of resource allocation in different areas of mental health services (including manpower resources, community support resources, and the degree of integration of primary services with mental hospitals' resources), and the public provision of preventive and health promotion services are considered to play a critical role in controlling the incidence and prevalence of mental disorders (WHO Atlas 2017). The available quantitative data (from secondary sources and publications), however, is deficient for undertaking a more comprehensive analysis that incorporates the availability of mental health care resources available to public and the efficiently that mental health services are delivered. Due to such limitations of comparable data, the study could not assess the effectiveness of a country's health system in relation to the mental health needs of the population.

In estimating PLSR, we employed SPSS and XLSTAT software. SPSS output of PLS regression generates five main tables: (i) proportion of variance explained (by latent factor); (ii) latent factor weights; (iii) latent factor loadings; (iv) independent variable importance in projection (VIP); and (v) regression parameter estimates (by dependent variable).

Tables 8 A, B, C, and D report the results using a cross section of data from OECD countries. Table 8A provides the SPSS output, "Proportion of Variance Explained by Latent Factors."

Table 8A. Proportion of Variance Explained
Statitics

Latent Factors	X Variance	Cumulative X Variance	Y Variance	Cumulative Y Variance (R-square)	Adjusted R-square
1	.319	.319	.545	.545	.528
2	.229	.548	.015	.559	.527
3	.110	.657	.005	.564	.514
4	.131	.788	6.668E-5	.564	.494
5	.105	.893	6.926E-6	.564	.473
6	.107	1.000	7.179E-7	.564	.450

In Table 8A, the column, the "cumulative X variance" is the percentage of variance in the X variables (the predictors) accounted for by the latent factors. The "cumulative Y variance" is the percentage of the variance in the Y variable(s) accounted for by the latent factors. In Table 8A, the adjusted R-square declines with increasing number of factors. We have retained only one latent factor and report detailed results in Table 8B based on the one latent factor.

Table 8B. Weights

Variables	Latent Factor 1
Gini wealth inequality	.554
EPL(employment protection)	−.350
Poverty youth	.374
Children with single parent	.345
Rent cost burden	.366
T20/B20(quintile ratio)	.422
Y variable	.538

X-weights in Table 8B represent the correlation/covariance of X variables with the Y-scores. The X-weights are used to calculate the X-scores. Table 8C represents how strongly each item is associated with the underlying factor. Typically, X-weights and X-loadings are similar in sign. From loadings in Table 8C, it is obvious that factor 1 is heavily associated with wealth inequality. By one rule of thumb in confirmatory PLS factor analysis is that loadings should be 0.7 or higher to confirm that independent variables identified a priori are represented by a particular factor. However, some researchers, particularly for exploratory purposes, use a lower level such as .4 for the central factor and .25 for other factors (Raubenheimer 2004, cited by Statnotes from North Carolina State University).

Table 8C. Loadings

Variables	Latent Factor 1
Gini wealth inequality	.569
EPL(employment protection)	–.314
Poverty youth	.474
Children with single parent	.297
Rent-cost burden	.382
T20/B20(quintile ratio)	.369
Y variable	1.000

Table 8D found below presents information on the model quality, variable importance in projection (VIP) coefficients, and regression parameter estimates. As mentioned below, VIP coefficients represent the importance of each X variable in fitting both the X- and Y-scores, since the Y-scores are predicted from the X-scores (Smart PLS 2016).

Table 8D. Model Quality and Variable Importance in Projection

Independent Variables (Predictors)	Model Quality	Variable Importance in Projection (VIP)	Parameters
Intercept			2.438
Wealth Inequality-(Gini)		1.356	0.003
Quintile Ratio(T20/B20)		1.035	0.016
Youth Poverty	Q2cum = 0.474 R2Y = 0.545 R2X = 0.319 MSE = 0.005 RMSE = 0.073	0.917	0.004
Housing Cost Burden		0.895	0.004
EPL (Employment Protection)		0.857	-0.032
Percentage of Children With Single Parent Household		0.844	0.004

Table 8D presents the results obtained from PLSR with one component from this table, it is evident that the computed model meets the goodness of fit requirements and predicts values close to the observed data values. All of the computed variables have expected signs. The goodness of fit of the model is given by R2 and Q2(cross-validated).[18] For a good predictive model, it is suggested that the root-mean squared error (RMSE) should be low (<0.3). High R2 and low RMSE are not sufficient indicators of model validity. For good predictability, it is recommended that the R2 – Q2 value should not exceed 0.3 (Verrasami et al. 2011).

Variable importance in projection (VIP) Score19: Partial Least Squares Model

VIP coefficients in Table 8D represent the importance of each X variable in fitting both the X- and Y-scores, since the Y-scores are predicted from the X-scores. The higher a variable's VIP score, the more influential it is in determining the PLSR model for both predictors and responses. Although VIP cut-off points vary throughout the literature, traditionally variables with VIP scores lower than 0.8 are deemed as non-influential in the model. As per the threshold set by Wold (1994) at 0.8, this study found the following variables to be the markers of social disadvantage: poverty, lower-social and economic status, poor employment conditions, family issues and housing issues. Parameter estimates are the regression coefficients, and the signs of the coefficients indicate the direction of the effect. In our estimates, all coefficients have expected signs. The estimated equation is as follows (See Table 8D).

Y=2.438+0.003 wealth inequality+0.016 income inequality+0.004 youth poverty +0.004 housing cost burden-0.032 EPL+0.004 percentage of children with single parent household

The following subsection explains the role of the above explanatory variables with support from the available cross-sectional evidence.

4.1 EXPLAINING THE EMPIRICAL FINDINGS

The findings of the present exercise are supported by the existing research evidence that mental health and many common mental disorders are shaped to a great extent by social and economic inequalities. As mentioned previously and emphasized in several studies, economic and social circumstances affect health through the physiological effects (relative income/status effect, Marmot and Williamson 2001) and material circumstances at the system level (public under-investments in education, social infrastructure, heath care, etc. Lynch et al. 2004). The PLSR results reported below highlight the role of socioeconomic structural factors (mainly upstream drivers) that affect the mental health of young people through relative and absolute deprivation pathways.

Poverty Status of Youth and Prevalence of Disorders

Youth poverty ranked the highest among the variable of importance in explaining mental illness. Data in Table 9 shows wide variations among OECD countries in terms of youth poverty rates, where the rate is substantially higher than the OECD average in Norway, USA, and Greece. Global estimates reveal that approximately 20% of adolescents and youth experience a mental health condition—such as depression, anxiety disorders, and disruptive behavioral disorders—each year, and those living in low-income countries make up 85–90% of this group (UN ESCAP 2014b).

The ILO's Future of Work Survey reported that many youths regarded the future (15 years ahead) either "with fear" or "with uncertainty"—and this response was more prevalent in developed countries (ILO 2017). Tables 9 and 10, compare data of youth poverty and prevalence of mental illness and indicate that youth in Norway, USA, and Greece have been experiencing higher rates of anxiety and depressive disorders than the youth in Slovenia, Czech Republic, Iceland, and Slovak republic, where youth poverty rates are much lower than the OECD average. The material well-being and mental health issues of youth call for action and remediation, since they lay the foundations for the future of a country's economy and prosperity.

Table 9. Poverty Rate (Relative to Threshold) among Youth (18–25) 2011, Selected Countries

Countries	Youth in Poverty (%)	Working Poor (%)
OECD Average	14	8.5
Norway	28.9	6.4
USA	21.6	11.7
Greece	21.6	14.1
Slovenia	5.1	5.7
Czech Republic	7.3	4.3
Iceland	7.3	5.3
Slovak Republic	7.4	5.9

Source: OECD (2014) (https://www.oecd.org/social/OECD2014-Income-Inequali-ty-Update.pdf).

Table 10. Prevalence of Mental disorders- Selected OECD Countries 2015

Countries	Anxiety disorders (% of population)	Depressive disorders (% of population)
OECD Average	NA	NA
Norway	4.7	7.4
USA	6.9	6.3
Greece	5.7	4.9
Slovenia	5.1	3.8
Czech Republic	5.2	3.8
Iceland	4.1	4.9
Slovak Republic	5.1	3.9

Source: WHO (2015): Depression and Other Common Mental Disorders Global Health Estimates.

Presence of Wealth Inequality and Mental Disorders

Since 1980, very large transfers of wealth from public to private sources occurred in nearly all countries, whether rich or emerging (World Inequality Report 2018). While national wealth substantially increased, public wealth is now negative or close to zero in rich countries, which limits the ability of governments to tackle inequality, resulting from wealth inequality among individuals. The 2018 report notes that wealth inequality among individuals has increased at different speeds across countries since 1980. This resulted in disproportionally unequal opportunities in access to education and well-paying jobs as well as stagnating or sluggish income growth rates of the poorest half of the population in countries.

Productivity growth ran ahead of real wage growth in the American economy for the last few decades, due to increased market power of the corporations (Stiglitz 2016). Real wage growth falling behind labor productivity growth results in the decline in the labor share in national income (arithmetically it means that labor share in national income is the same as real wage/marginal product of labor; Solow 2014). A growing body of evidence in recent years suggests that labor shares have shown a secular downward trend with important negative consequences (OECD 2015). As a result, the capital share has risen and the labor share fallen (Solow 2014).

Studies have shown that a decrease in the share of total market income from wages and other labor compensation, as well as an increase in the share from capital gains contribute to the increase in market income inequality because capital gains are much more concentrated among higher-income households than labor income (Congressional Budget Office 2011). Over time and across many countries, a higher capital share has been associated with higher inequality in the personal distribution of income (Piketty 2013). According to Piketty's analysis, the size of the gap between r (rate of return on capital) and g (the economy's growth rate) is one of the important forces that account for the magnitude and variations in wealth inequality in the end. The gap between r and g will tend to amplify the steady-state inequality of a wealth distribution that arises out of a given mixture of shocks (including labor income shocks; Piketty 2015).[20]

Based on Piketty's findings on wealth distribution and from the CSDH report, Marmot (2014b) remarks, "Social injustice is killing on a grand scale." To explain the link between wealth inequalities and mental health risk, Wilkinson and Pickett (2017) maintain that we all worry more about how others see us and judge our status. In psychological jargon, this is termed as "social evaluation threat." Increased "social evaluative" threats make social life more stressful, since we all need to feel valued. Stress hormones respond significantly to social evaluation anxieties. Using the brain's "dominance behavioral system" model, Johnson, Leedom, and Muhtadie (2012) remarked that anxiety and depression were related to subordination and submissiveness, as well as a desire to avoid subordination. That is, the number of mental illnesses and personality disorders were linked to issues of dominance and sub- ordination exacerbated by inequality.

Based on the evidence, Wilkinson and Pickett (2017) argued that in a more unequal society, status anxiety increased not just among the poor, but also across all income deciles. These authors further remarked that depression, schizophrenia, narcissism, and psychotic symptoms all more commonly appeared in more unequal societies. Nowatzki (2012), in a bivariate cross-sectional analysis of the relationship between wealth inequality (Gini coefficient) and population health (life expectancy and infant mortality) in 14 wealthy countries confirmed that wealth inequality is associated with poor population health.

The inspection of the data Table 11 gives some visual evidence of association between extreme wealth inequalities and the prevalence of mental disorders (age standardized) for some countries included in this study. This ostensible evidence corroborates the view that more disparities in the possession of wealth between rich and poor may exert a greater influence on mental health than less dis- parities. For example, the countries with extreme wealth inequalities— the United States, Sweden, and Chile—also have higher prevalence rates of mental disorders compared to Slovenia and Slovakia—the countries with relatively less wealth inequalities.

Role of Income Disparities

Gini coefficient is often chosen as measures of inequality. However, researchers analyzing the effects of inequality employ several different measures, guided by the focus of the research. Income distribution data by deciles for OECD countries show that while the income of the top quintile rose faster over time, the bottom quintile experienced the least growth of income. By using sensitivity analyses, decile ratios allowed researchers to examine which sections of the income spectrum could be most important as a social determinant of health (De Maio 2007). However, Gini coefficient does not identify which parts of the income distribution are most responsible for the measured inequality. Another disadvantage of the Gini coefficient is that there is no unique map- ping between changes in the Gini index and the underlying income distributions (Deininger and Squire 1996). For example, a redistribution from the top to the middle class may be associated with the same change in the aggregate indicator as an increase in the share of income received by the bottom at the expense of the middle class. To overcome this shortcoming, and to uncover possible movements in the income received by the individual groups in the society, Deininger and Squire (1996) recommended using additional measures, such as income shares by quintile, wherever possible (p. 567).

Table 11. Wealth Inequality (Gini coefficient) 2016 and Prevalence of Mental Disorders: Data Relating to Extreme Cases of Countries

Countries	Wealth Gini coefficient 2016	Mental and substance use disorders, Age standardized prevalence rate (%) 2015
USA	86.2	21.557
UK	73.2	17.6
Sweden	83.2	18.193
Slovenia	58.5	14.947
Slovakia	49	14.49
Norway	79.8	18.17
Japan	63.1	14.08
Denmark	89.3	16.458
Chile	80.5	19.07
Canada	73.2	18.95

Source: Global Wealth Data—book 2016, Credit Suisse Wealth Report; Hannah Ritchie and Max Roser (2018)—Mental Health. Published online at OurWorldInData. org. Retrieved from: https://ourworldindata.org/mental-health.

Income quintile ratio (IQR) is the average income of the richest 20% of the population to the average income of the poorest 20% of the population. The IQR removes the middle incomes from the equation, a sector of the population that tends to obscure poverty in other measures like the Gini Index. The present study used IQR as a predictor of M&SUD.

Growth in inequality is fueled not only by increasing capital income ratios but also by the growth of top incomes (comments by Solow 2014 on Piketty). Top incomes are growing rapidly in most advanced countries, while people at the bottom are unemployed or languishing on insecure, part-time, and low-paid work. Regarding the earned income differences, the top executives have concentrated their efforts on securing a larger share of profits (in response to cuts in top tax rates) due to the increased bargaining power rather than increased productive efforts in the direction of enterprise growth and employment (Alverodo et al. 2013; Stiglitz 2016). These large pay packages are converted to wealth and future income from wealth (Solow 2014).

Table 12 reports the data on quintile ratio and M&SUD for a sample of countries with extreme ends in income disparities (e.g., Chile, USA, and Spain versus Slovak Republic and Slovenia). Those countries showing higher quintile ratio than the world OECD average also tend to have a higher prevalence of mental illness than the world average, while those with lower quintile ratio tend to have a lower prevalence than average. This anecdotal evidence is consistent with the findings reported by Pickett, James, and Wilkinson (2006), in their international analysis on the association between income inequality (quin- tile ratio) and the prevalence of mental illness. They found a strong ($r=0.73$) and significant (p value=0.04) linear correlation between the prevalence of any mental illness and income inequality and between serious mental illness and income inequality ($r=0.74$, p value=0.03). Patel et al. (2018) in their systematic review of 26 studies, mostly from high-income countries, found that nearly two-thirds of all studies and five out of six longitudinal studies reported a statistically significant positive relationship between income inequality and risk of depression; only one study reported a statistically significant negative relationship. Evidence suggests that more-egalitarian societies are more cohesive and better integrated into a network of social relations known to benefit health than less egalitarian societies (Wilkinson 2000).

Table 12. Quintile Ratio and Prevalence of Mental and Substance-Use Disorders. Selected Sample of Countries

Countries	Quintile Ratio (2014)	Prevalence of Mental and Substance use disorders (Age standardized) % 2015
Chile	10.6	19.07
USA	8.7	21.5
Spain	6.7	18.33
Greece	6.3	17.48
UK	6.0	17.6
Australia	5.7	21.62
Canada	5.5	18.95
Slovak Republic	4.1	14.57
Slovenia	3.8	14.94
Czech Republic	3.7	14.57
Denmark	3.6	16.45
Iceland	3.4	16.48
OECD	5.1	
World		15.47

Source for Quintile Ratio: OECD income distribution databases. For Prevalence of Mental and Substance use (age Standardized): Hannah Ritchie and Max Roser (2018)—"Mental Health." Published online at OurWorldInData.org.

The Impact of Housing Cost Burden

Housing costs can be a substantial financial burden on households, especially for low-income households. The median of the ratio of housing cost over income gives an indication of the financial pressure that households face due to housing costs. People in households that spend 30% or more of total household income on shelter expenses are defined as having a "housing affordability" problem. Another common measure for housing affordability by OECD is the "housing cost overburden rate," which measures the proportion of households or population that spend more than 40% (following the Eurostat methodology) of their disposable income on housing cost. Inadequate housing, including structural housing quality and overcrowding, is associated with increased risk of common mental disorders in adults (Lund et al. 2018).

Evidence from several research studies suggests that suitable housing arrangements in the community for people with severe mental illness can reduce hospital admissions. Poor housing affordability can result in homelessness that is likely to be both a consequence and a determinant of poor mental health (Bentley et al. 2011). These authors further added that affordability could influence health via the quality location and tenure of dwellings that households have access to. Persons with improper or lack of housing facilities experience significant barriers to self-care and personal hygiene, including limited access to clean showers, laundry, and handwashing facilities. Access to good-quality, afford- able housing is a key to achieving a number of social policy objectives, including reduction of poverty and enhancement of equality of opportunity, social inclusion, and mobility. Evidence shows that a significant number of people across OECD countries are homeless and too many households live in low-quality dwellings or face housing costs they can ill afford (OECD Affordable Housing Database).

Juxtaposing data on rent paid by bottom quintile (i.e., the 20% of the population with the lowest income) and prevalence of M&SUD, as in Table 13, we observe some (bare eye) evidence of a positive association between high percentage of rental cost and the high prevalence of mental illness in countries compared to the world average. In some of the central and eastern European countries (CEECs), where the rent cost burden is below 30%, the prevalence of M&SUD is also observed to be well below the world average. The median burden of rent payments for tenant households is highest in Norway (32.1%) and lowest for CEECs. In Chile, Greece, and the United States, households in the bottom quintile of the income distribution face housing costs that make up half or more of their income. Yet, in most of countries, low-income tenant households face median housing costs between 20% and 45% of their income.

It is estimated that providing permanent supportive housing to the homeless community saves the taxpayer money: reduces health care costs by 59%, reduces emergency department costs by 61%, and decreases the number of general inpatient hospitalizations by 77% (Garrett 2012). The Mental Health Commission of Canada in its final report (2014), estimated that "for every $1 spent providing housing and support for a homeless person with severe mental illness, $2.17 in savings are reaped because that person spends less time in hospital, prison, and in shelters".

Table 13. Housing Cost Burden and Mental Illness

Countries	Rent (private and subsidized) Bottom quintile	Prevalence of Mental and substance use Disorders Age Standardized 2015 (% of population)
Chile	83.30%	19.0788
Greece	54.55%	17.49
United States	50.00%	21.55
Spain	46.90%	18.33
United Kingdom	42.40%	17.55
Sweden	41.61%	18.19
Czech Republic	39.57%	14.576
Canada	38.62%	18.95
Finland	38.59%	18.88
Belgium	36.79%	17.77
Poland	24.32%	14.21
Slovenia	21.02%	14.947
Slovak Republic	19.34%	14.49
Hungary	18.10%	14.57
Ireland	15.94%	16.48
Bulgaria	12.14%	14.04
World		15.45

Note: Median of rent burden (private market and subsidized rent) as a share of disposable income in the bottom quintile of the income distribution (i.e., the 20% of the population with the lowest income). This is labeled as HC1.2.2. in

OECD data reporting. *The data on the prevalence of mental and substance-use disorders (age standardized) as a percentage of population is taken from Hannah Ritchie and Max Roser (2018)—"Mental Health." Published online at OurWorldInData.org.*

The Impact of Precarious Employment on Mental Health

As mentioned earlier that one of the most important factors shaping people's social position and mental happiness include employment, income and working conditions. However, labor market developments in the past few decades have made it more difficult for young adults to attain the economic stability and self-sufficiency that are important markers of the transition to adulthood (Danziger and Ratner 2010). The nature of prevailing employment conditions is now affected by the power relationships between employers and employees (Benach et al 2014). The declining proportion of union members among employees and resulting weakening of collective bargaining systems has been accompanied by the growth of non-standard work contracts or precarious jobs in the past few decades (OECD 2019). Precarious employment is considered a risk factor for mental health. Vives et al. (2013) reported a gradient association between employment precariousness and poor mental health, which was somewhat stronger among women, suggesting an interaction with gender-related power asymmetries.[21] In a study of Italian workers, Moscone et al. (2016) showed that the probability of psychotropic medication prescription was higher for workers under temporary job contracts. In a study of Southern Ontario by McMaster University (2015), covering over 4,000 workers between the ages of 25 and 65 years, precarious work led to anxiety and stress, affected social relationships, and diminished com- munity connections. Many empirical studies exploring employment precarity and its association with mental health focused on the dimension of job insecurity (Benach and Mutainer 2007). These studies found employment insecurity to be associated with poorer health (Lewchuk et al. 2003). Another dimension of precariousness is the degree of regulatory protection—that is, whether the worker has access to an equivalent level of regulatory protection through union representation or the law (Cranford et al. 2003).

The legislation governing termination of employment (like labor protection legislation) reflects labor market conditions in a given period. The Employment Protection Legislation (EPL)22 index is considered at best an approximate indicator of differences in some particular elements of employment law that are only one of several determinants of employment practice. Evidence from OECD income inequality studies reveal that less strict EPL is associated with greater wage dispersion, driven entirely by reforms to EPL for temporary workers (OECD 2011b).

The EMP indicator appeared as a variable of importance associated with mental disorders in our PLS. Table 14 shows wide variations among OECD countries in regard to the regulatory protection of temporary forms of employment. Pairing mental illness data with the regulatory protection of temporary workers index, we observe negative association with lower level of employment protection and mental health across the sample countries. Canada and the United States are countries with extremely lax labor market regulations. Poland, Slovenia, and Czech Republic fall on the other end of the spectrum.

Table 14. Regulatory Protection of Temporary Forms of Employment and Mental and Substance-Use Disorders (Sample of Selected Countries Showing Extreme End Variation in Regulatory Protection Index)

Countries	Regulation on temporary forms of employment 2013	Prevalence of Mental and Substance abuse disorders 2015
Canada	0.21	18.95
USA	0.33	21.55
UK	0.54	17.6
New-Zealand	0.92	18.4
Australia	1.04	21.62
Sweden	1.17	18.19
Netherlands	1.17	18.4
Norway	3.42	18.17
France	3.75	18.49
Slovak Republic	2.42	14.49
Poland	2.33	14.21
Slovenia	2.13	14.94
Czech Republic	2.13	14.57
World Average		15.47

Source for Regulation on Temporary forms of employment, OECD databases. For Prevalence of Mental and Substance use (Age Standardized): Hannah Ritchie and Max Roser (2018)—"Mental Health." Published online at OurWorldInData.org.

In the last two decades, easing of labor market regulations (lax hiring and firing), as well as changing power relationships in employment and wage bargaining, has resulted in higher market inequality (Debra-Morris et al. 2015; ILO 2015b;) estimated that easing of labor market regulations associated with higher market inequality and income share of the top 10%. Analyzing the effects of financial crisis and recession on mental health of the people, Karanikolos et al. (2013) suggested the positive role of social protection policies in mitigating the adverse consequences. These authors cited the experiences of Finland and Sweden, where at least $300 per person was spent during financial crisis and contend that social-welfare spending rather than general government spending significantly reduced mortality from diseases related to social circumstances (such as alcohol-related deaths).

Effects of Family Structure on Mental Health of Children

Both falling marriage rates and increasing divorce rates (OECD 2010a, SF3.1) contributed to the increase in single-parent families (OECD 2011). Household formation is mentioned as one of the factors driving dispersion of household labor income (OECD 2012, Ch. 5). Child well-being is related to family structure, family resources, and public policies promoting children's material well-being. There are more single-headed households with and without children today than ever before: the share of working-age households increased in all OECD countries, from an average of 15% in the late 1980s to 20% in the mid-2000s. On average, it is found that the poverty rate for single parents (at 32%) was three times higher than for all families with children (Förster and d'Ercole 2005). Lone parents and their children experience higher than average levels of adverse health and social outcomes, many of which are explained by high rates of poverty (Bramlett and Blumberg 2007; Campbell et al. 2016; Gucciardi, Celasun, and Stewart 2004).

A number of studies have documented that children in families who experienced homelessness frequently became separated from their parents (Shinn, Gibbons-Benton, and Brown 2015). Children of a single mother are, on average, poorer, less educated, and have fewer prospects—an underclass in a wealthy and aging nation that can ill-afford to lose a significant chunk of its future workforce. Single-parent families have disproportionately higher rates of low-wage (less than two-thirds of the median wage) employment. Good family relations, with good parenting behaviors, are conducive to well-functioning parents and children. Single-parent families and their high poverty rates remain a vexing concern in OECD countries. Psychiatric disorders have been found to occur with higher frequency in children of single-parent families, especially those lacking a father during the child's whole life (Moilanen and Rantakallio 1988). These authors further add that childhood enuresis was most frequent in children who experienced the divorce of their parents.

APPENDIX TO CH 4: PARTIAL LEAST SQUARE REGRESSION APPROACH

PLSR is an acronym which originally stood for partial least squares regression (Abdi 2010). PLSR, also known as Projection to Latent Structures, is a popular approach for analyzing high-dimensional data, viz., relating to problems in bioinformatics and genomics. PLSR was originally developed for econometrics to deal with collinear predictor variables. PLSR is a method for constructing predictive models when the factors are many and highly collinear (Tobias 2016). PLSR generalizes and combines features from principal component analysis and multiple regression. Its goal is to predict or analyze a set of dependent variables from a set of independent variables or predictors by extracting from the predictors a set of orthogonal factors called latent variables that have the best predictive power (Abdi 2007). In nutshell, the X variables (the predictors) in PLSR are reduced to principal components, as are the Y variables (the dependents). The components of X are used to predict the scores on the Y components, and the predicted Y component scores are used to predict the actual values of the Y variables.

Both principal component regression (PCR) and PLSR techniques circumvent this by decomposing X into orthogonal scores and loadings. The major difference between PCR and PLSR is, while PCR uses only the variation of to construct new factors, PLSR uses both the variation of and to construct new factors that play the role of explanatory variables (Yeniay and Goktas 2002).[37] The principle behind PLSR is to search for a set of latent vectors by performing a simultaneous decomposition of X and Y with the constraint that these components explain as much as possible of the covariance between X and Y (Zhao et al. 2013). That is, PLSR estimates regression parameters so that the variance of Y explained the explanatory variables are maximal. Assume is an n ×p matrix of predictor (independent) variables and is a n×q matrix (of dependent or response variables). The PLSR technique works by successively extracting factors from both X and Y such that covariance between the extracted factors is maximized. Both X and Y are decomposed into scores and loadings in such a way that the covariance between and scores is maximized. Partial least squares do not need the data to come from normal or known distributions (Falk and Miller 1992).

To regress the Y variables with the explanatory variables $X1,...,Xp$, PLSR attempts to find latent variables or components that play the same role as the Xs (Yeniay and Goktas 2002). Assume is an n ×p matrix of predictor (independent) variables and is an n×q matrix (of dependent or response variables). The PLSR technique works by successively extracting factors from both X and Y such that covariance between the extracted factors is maximized. Partial least squares regression is based on the basic latent component decomposition (Boulesteix and Strimmer 2007) as shown in equations (1) and (2). That is, the PLSR technique tries to find a linear decomposition of X and Y such that

$$X = TP^T + E \qquad (1)$$

$$Y = UQ^T + F \qquad (2)$$

The matrix X is decomposed into a matrix T (the score matrix) and a matrix P (the loadings matrix) plus an error matrix E. The matrix Y is decomposed into U (score matrix), Q (the loadings matrix), and the error term F. These two equations are called outer relations (Geladi and Kowalski 1986). The extracted factors (T) are used to predict the Y-scores (U), and then the predicted Y-scores are used to construct pre- dictions for the responses (Tobias 2016).

Decomposition is finalized to maximize covariance between T and U. There are multiple algorithms available to solve the PLSR problem. However, all algorithms follow an iterative process to extract the X-scores and Y-scores. (See details in Abdi 2010; Maitra and Yan 2008).

5. MENTAL HEALTH CARE: CHALLENGES AND RESOURCE-GAPS IN COUNTRIES

Research studies have drawn attention to the important role of the health system in mediating the differential consequences of illness in people's lives (Solar and Irwin 2010). Despite the fact that mental and behavioral disorders account for one of the largest and fastest-growing categories of the burden of disease, evidence shows that the global response of the countries' health systems to meet mental health-related challenges has remained quite meek, and there persists still today, a wide wedge between evidence-based effective policies and the prevailing practices among countries (Vigo et al. 2016). In its Mental Health Atlas report, the WHO (2011) indicated that the availability of mental health care resources varied significantly across countries. The present study attempted to use the number of psychiatrists per 100,000 members of the population as a proxy explanatory variable to represent health system resources. This variable could not meet the threshold criterion.

It needs to be pointed out that there are diverse dimensions of every country's health system that are difficult to capture due to data avail- ability issues. A mental health system is a multifaceted system with wide variations among countries in several respects—viz., in terms of public health priority and funding designated to the mental health sector, timely and affordable access to mental health care services, practice of evidence-based quality treatment, availability of community resources, division of resources between institutionalized versus community-based residential facilities, and the degree of coordination between primary and secondary mental health hospitals. More research is needed to develop suitable indicators that represent the significance of the health resources and people's mental health care needs.

From the policy perspective, some areas of a health system warrant priority attention. The following discussion focuses on key issues impinging the health system in most countries.

5.1 PROBLEM OF DEFICIENT RESOURCES IN RELATION TO NEEDS

Mental health care has remained grossly underfunded worldwide. In many countries around the globe, spending on mental health represents less than 1% of health expenditures nationally. The number of psychiatrists, nurses, and psychologists per 100,000 members of the population is inadequate given the increasing need for mental health care services. WHO's 2017 *Mental Health Atlas* reports that in more than two-thirds of countries, care and treatment of persons with severe mental disorders is not included in national health insurance or reimbursement schemes (WHO 2017). Mental hospitals (specialized, independent, and stand- alone facilities) represent the primary mode of inpatient service in 80% of countries (Morris et al. 2012), and the transition to community care remains a huge challenge in both developed and developing countries. The Mental Health Atlas also reveals that although some countries have made progress in mental health policymaking and planning, there is a widespread global shortage of health workers trained in mental health and a lack of investment in community-based mental health facilities.

5.2 DEARTH OF EPIDEMIOLOGICAL DATABASES—A BARRIER TO EVIDENCE-BASED PRACTICES

Barring the United States and a few other nations, there are negligible efforts in the direction of ecological[23] and epidemiological[24] research studies in many countries (Wittchen et al. 2011). There is also a lack of longitudinal studies needed to build public-use databases with comprehensive information on both social factors and health, collected over periods long enough—ideally multiple generations—for health consequences of early childhood experiences to manifest

(Braveman, Egerter, and Williams 2011). Even for disorders that are widely prevalent, such as depression, there is a scarcity of data related to treatment in OECD countries (Armesto, Medeiros, and Wei 2008). Mental health information systems are the building blocks of a health system and consistently provide accurate information enabling planning and evaluation of mental health service delivery (WHO 2004b).

OECD (2014) states that the availability of data and information in the following areas needs to be improved:

1. Data on prevalence of mental illness and the need for mental health care services, as determined by epidemiologic surveys; indicators of readmission rates.
2. Indicators of inpatient suicide or suicide after discharge (treatment outcomes indicator).
3. Indicators of premature death because of severe mental illness (treatment outcome indicator).
4. Primary care indicators (for treatment of mild-to-moderate mental disorders).
5. Quality measures related to social outcomes (such as improved participation in the labor market or education).

An effective surveillance system that provides ongoing comprehensive and timely information on the entire spectrum of the mental health population is needed. Although many OECD countries have made considerable progress in benchmarking the quality and outcomes of mental health care systems, these initiatives have still posed substantial challenges for cross-country comparisons.

5.3 LACK OF INTEGRATION OF MENTAL HEALTH SERVICES INTO PRIMARY HEALTH CARE

Abundant research-based evidence indicates that when mental health care is integrated into primary care, the integration results in many benefits: narrowing of the treatment gap by reducing stigma;

enhanced access to mental health care services delivered closer to people's homes; and the provision of mental health care that is affordable, timely, and cost-effective (WHO and WONCA 2008). An integrated and community-based model is more appropriate to treat people with comorbid long-term conditions (Saxena et al. 2007; Thornicroft, Deb, and Henderson 2016).

Many developed countries concerned with restraining the growth of public health expenditures and challenges related to the shortages of human and hospital resources, have adopted the practice of assigning the "gate keeping" role to primary care physicians (PCPs). There are complaints that patients experience longer delays and frustrations within this practice. Many studies have emphasized that specialty-referral process needs to be improved (Foot, Naylor, and Imison 2010; Forest et al. 2006; Malhotra et al. 2011). Studies have reported that referring clinicians and specialists exchange information less frequently than necessary, and this has adverse consequences for patients (Forrest et al. 2000). There are also controversies about the gate-keeping role of PCPs (Bodenheimer and Casalino 1999; Grumbach and Damberg 1999). It is recommended that PCPs be transformed from gatekeepers into coordinators of care, in which the goal of the PCP is to integrate both primary and specialty care to improve overall quality of care (Bodenheimer and Casalino 1999). In many countries, health care professionals in primary care do not have comprehensive training to diagnose, treat, and manage mental illness, as well as the continuing professional development and guidelines that can ensure practitioners are up-to-date on evidence-based best practices (OECD 2014a).

6. SUBSTANCE USE DISORDERS AND MENTAL ILLNESS

Mental illnesses and substance use often occur together (Drake, Mueser, & Brunette 2007).[25] Both alcohol and SUDs have common and overlapping risk factors (Degenhardt and Hall 2012), such as stress, trauma, adverse childhood events, epigenetic influences and others (NIDA 2018). There is consistent evidence of frequent association of alcohol consumption with the use of other psychoactive substances, particularly with opioids and benzodiazepines (Peacock et al 2018, GBD 2016 Alcohol and Drug Use Collaborators Lancet 2018). Establishing causality or directionality is difficult, that is, comorbidity between substance use disorders and other mental illnesses does not necessarily mean that one caused the other, even if one appeared first (NIDA 2018). National epidemiologic surveys and numerous clinical studies consistently indicate that SUDs and mood and anxiety disorders have strong interrelations when considered on a lifetime basis (Grant et al 2004).

Mental illness is common among people who struggle with substance abuse and addiction (SAMSHA 2017). Chronic use of some drugs can lead to both short- and long-term changes in the brain, which can lead to mental health issues including paranoia, depression, anxiety, aggression, hallucinations, and other problems (NIDA 2017). Evidence from U.S. research shows that, compared with the general population, people addicted to substance use are roughly twice as likely to suffer from mood and anxiety disorders, with the reverse also true(NIDA 2017). In a longitudinal study that followed 45,000 young Swedish soldiers for 15 years, it was found that those who smoked marijuana were more than twice as likely to develop schizophrenia (Andréasson et al.1987). SUD occurs when a person's use of alcohol or another substance leads to health issues or problems at work, school, or home (US Library of Medicine, Medical Encyclopedia).

Studies also suggest the reverse causation that people who are diagnosed with mood or anxiety disorders are nearly twice as likely to have a SUD compared to the general public (NIDA 2010). Evidence plausibly has ascertained that certain mental disorders such as affective and anxiety disorders may precede the development of substance abuse problems.

Both, alcohol and drugs are major global risk factors for disability and premature loss of life. The overuse of these substances results in adverse and serious social consequences in the form of serious road injuries, educational failure and drop out, juvenile crime, and treatment and rehabilitation cost to the public. As of 2008, alcohol use accounted for 53.9% of total substance use, followed by cannabis (18.0%), opioids (14.5%), and cocaine (7.9%) (WHO Atlas 2010).

The following subsection presents a review of the prevalence and disease burden attributable to alcohol and drug use across world regions and over a time span of 2000-2016.

6.1 ALCOHOL USE INCIDENCE, PREVALENCE AND DISORDERS

Alcohol is a psychoactive substance with dependence-producing properties (WHO 2014). The 2016 GBD study (GBD 2016 Alcohol Collaborators, 2018) has produced detailed evidence on alcohol and drug use and disorder in 195 countries. The following broad observations have been reported by this study. First, among all the psychoactive substance uses, alcohol use disorders (AUDs) have been found to be the most prevalent as of 2016, with age-standardized prevalence of 1320.8 cases per 100,000 people, followed by cannabis dependence as the next most common drug use disorders (DUDs), with age-standardized prevalence of 289.7 cases per 100,000 people. It is observed by comparing Tables 15 and 17 that the prevalence of AUDs totaled to 100,389.2 thousands compared to 63,668.5 thousands in the case of drug use in 2016 (GBD 2016 Alcohol and Drug Use Collaborator, 2018). Second, it has been noted that that among the population aged 15–49 years, alcohol use was the leading risk factor globally in 2016, with 3.8% of female deaths and 12.2% of male deaths in that age group attributable to alcohol use (GBD 2016 Alcohol collaborators, 2018). Third, alcohol use ranked as the seventh leading risk factor globally for premature death and dis- ability in 2016, compared with other risk factors in the GBD studies. For men, alcohol use has been found as the fourth leading risk factor causing early death and disability in 2017 (Institute for Health Metrics and Evaluation IHME, 2018).

Globally, alcohol was the most prevalent substance of dependence (Peacock et al 2018). AUDs are comprised of alcohol dependence and the harmful use of alcohol (ATLAS on substance use 2010, WHO). There is a causal relationship between harmful use of alcohol and a range of mental and behavioral disorders, other non-communicable conditions as well as injuries (WHO 2018). Another daunting finding is that alcohol abuse and dependence had the widest treatment gap at 78.1% (Kohn et al 2004) among mental and substance use disorders.

Beyond health consequences, the harmful use of alcohol brings significant social and economic losses to individuals and society at large (WHO 2018). DALYs represent a measure of overall disease burden, quantifying mortality and morbidity due to alcohol and illicit drug use in a single disease measure. The burden of disease expressed in DALYs quantifies the gap between the current health status of the population and an ideal situation where everyone lives to old age in full health (WHO, 2009a). Unintentional injuries, digestive diseases and AUDs were the leading contributors to the burden of disease and injury caused by alcohol and were individually responsible for 30.0%, 17.6% and 13.9% of all alcohol attributable DALYs. The acute consumption of alcohol has also been shown to affect a number of cognitive functions, including planning, verbal fluency, memory and complex motor control. These deficits in cognitive functions may increase the risk of injury (WHO 2018). In 2016, the leading contributors to the burden of alcohol attributable deaths and DALYs among men were injuries, digestive diseases, and AUDs, whereas among women the leading contributors were cardiovascular diseases, digestive diseases, and injuries (WHO 2018). Global DALYs attributable to alcohol use were highest for injuries, cardiovascular diseases, and cancers (GBD 2016 Table 3). Table 15 below reveal near stagnation in the cases of AUDs in terms of YLD over the last two and half decades.

Table 15. Alcohol Use: Incidence, Prevalence and Disease Burden 2016

Disease	Incidence thousands	Prevalence thousands	Disease Burden (YLD) in thousands	Percentage Change in YLD 2006-2016	Percentage change in age-standardized rates between 2006 and 2016
Alcohol Use Disorders	50432	100389	10031	9.7	-4.8

Source: GBD 2016 Disease and Injury Incidence and Prevalence Collaborators (2017)

Regional Variations in Alcohol Use Disorders

Alcohol is consumed by more than half of the population in only three WHO regions – the Americas, Europe and the Western Pacific (WHO 2018, Global Status Report on Alcohol 2018). The highest levels of per capita alcohol consumption are observed in countries of the WHO European Region (WHO 2018, GBD 2016 Disease and Injury Incidence and Prevalence Collaborators, Lancet 2017). Within the European region, the Central, Eastern and Western Europe recorded consistently higher alcohol consumption per capita (11.64, 11.55 and 11.13 liters, respectively) and a higher percentage of heavy consumption among consumers (49.5%, 46.9% and 40.2%, respectively) (Peacock et al 2018). Degenhardt et al (2016), in their comparative study of substance abuse found that alcohol has caused most health burden in Eastern Europe. From 2000 to 2016 however, the European Region as a whole experienced a moderate reduction in consumption per capita from 12.3 liters in 2005 to 9.8 liters in 2016. Worldwide, 44.8% of total recorded alcohol is consumed in the form of spirits, followed by beer (34.3%) and by wine (11.7%). Spirits are the leading drink in Eastern Europe, Central and Northern America and most of Asia. Spirits contain 40% of pure alcohol equivalent, compared to just 11-16 % in wine and 4-5% in beer (OECD Health Statistics 2018).

The following Table 16 provides a snapshot of the alcohol use related disease burden across regions at two points in time, 2001 and 2016. As observed from the table, the disease burden increased in all world regions with the exception of Africa and Europe, though Europe experienced the highest alcohol attributable DALYs. In terms of absolute burden, the Lancet's GBD Alcohol Collaborators study estimated the largest number of alcohol-attributable DALYs in East Asia, South Asia, Eastern Europe, and Tropical Latin America in 2016 (GBD 2016). According to these findings, prevalence of these disorders has been the highest for countries and regions with high social development index (SDI).[26]

Table 16. Regional Profile of Alcohol Use Disorders: All age Groups, 2000–2016

Regions	2000 **AUD** DALYs(%)	2016 **AUD** DALYs(%)
AFR	7.3	6.27
AMR	9.98	13.0
EMR	2.53	5.04
EUR	20.6	18.45
SEAR	5.7	9.0
WPR	6.67	8.4
World	9.4	10.7

Source: Data Compiled from WHO Disease Burden Databases

In addition to the higher vulnerability of people in the adolescence age, national laws and policies, socioeconomic inequalities and community factors influence the prevalence of addictive behavior.

Drugs Use and the Associated Disease Burden

Global estimates from 2012 indicate that around 5.2% (range: 3.5- 7.0%) of the world population aged 15-64 had used an illicit drug — mainly a substance belonging to the cannabis, opioid, cocaine or amphetamine type stimulant (ATS) group — at least once in the previous year (UNODC 2014). Drug use disorders have been observed to cause higher disease burden than alcohol at the global level. As of 2016, the WHO databases show that in comparison to AUDs, drug use has been found to result in both higher deaths (1.25 times that of AUDs) and YLDs (14597 thousands for drugs versus 12655 for AUDs). It is estimated that of the total DALYs attributable to NCDs, the DALYs related to DUDs contributed more than 2.25% compared to the contribution of just 1.5% from AUDs in 2016 (GBD 2016 Disease and Injury Incidence and Prevalence Collaborators, Lancet 2017).

Table 17. Drugs Use: Incidence, Prevalence and Disease Burden 2016

Disease	Incidence thousands	Prevalence thousands	Disease Burden (YLD) in thousands	Percentage Change in YLD 2006-2016	Percentage change in age-standardized rates between 2006 and 2016
Drug Use Disorders	7460	61968	14607	15.5	1.4

Source: GBD 2016 Disease and Injury Incidence and Prevalence Collaborators (2017)

Illicit drugs use can have a profoundly negative effect on health in the form of premature death, severely curtailing the quality of life through disability (any short-term or long-term health loss), such as from liver disease, or infection with HIV and hepatitis B and C as a result of sharing contaminated needles (UNODC 2014). In the long run the dependence on drugs causes social dysfunction, unemployment, disability, and death. Results from multiple sources indicate that the development of illicit drug dependence among users generate some common pattern of problems (Degenhardt et al., 2010, Toumbourou et al., 2007): earlier onset of drug use; use of more types of illicit drugs; and onset before age 15 of externalizing (e.g. conduct disorder) and internalizing mental disorders (e.g. depression).

Among drug disorders, opioids contributed 87% of YLDs and 76% of DALYs in 2016 (Degenhardt & Patton, GBD 2016 Alcohol and Drug Use Collaborators 2018). For these two most commonly used drugs, cannabis and opioid, estimates of dependence show that there were 19.8 and 16.8 million cases in 2015, respectively (Peacock et al 2018). Comparing the probable adverse health consequences of problem use of amphetamines, cannabis, cocaine, and opioids, Degenhardt & Hall (2012) remark that while cannabis contributes little to mortality, the major adverse health effects of cannabis use are dependence and probably psychotic disorders and other mental disorders.

Regional Variations in Prevalence of Drug Use Disorders

Table 18 below, reporting DALYs from DUDs for two points in time, 2000 and 2016 in all regions of the world. It depicts an increase in mental disorder DALYs attributable to drug use, with the Americas showing the largest increase, and the largest burden. Degenhardt et al (2016), in their comparative analysis of substance abuse disorder, found that the illicit drug burden has been relatively higher in the United States, Canada, Australia, New Zealand, and western Europe compared to alcohol use disorders. The regions with highest drug attributable burdens included Eastern Europe (1252.3 age standardized

DALYs per 100,000 people) and high-income North America (1380.3 age-standardized DALYs per 100,000 people) in 2016 (GBD 2016 Alcohol Collaborators, Lancet 2018, P997). The EMR (Eastern Mediterranean Region) ranks next to Americas in terms of the burden from drug use disorders. In terms of absolute burden, the largest number of drug-attributable DALYs were in East Asia, high-income North America, South Asia, and Eastern Europe.

In the region of Americas, data show that, with the exception of opiates, the use of all other groups of substances (cannabis, opioids, cocaine, ATS and "ecstasy") have remained at levels higher than the global average in the region between 2002 and 2012 (UNODC 2014, UNODC 2017). In Europe, cannabis is by far the most commonly consumed illicit substance, with estimated users comprising 4.3% of those aged 15-64, followed by cocaine (UNODC 2014). The use of opioids and opiates is comparable to global average levels (UNODC 2014). Overall, the use cannabis has the highest prevalence in North America, Western Europe and Oceania. According to the American Academy of Child and Adolescent Psychiatry (updated information, May 2018, number 106), teenage marijuana use is at its highest level in 30 years, and today's teens are more likely to use marijuana than tobacco. Evidence also confirms that legalization of medical and recreational marijuana in some U.S. states and other countries has increased the accessibility and appeal of the drug to youth. The use of cocaine has been largely concentrated in North America, followed by Western and Central Europe, and South America (UNODC 2009).

The prevalence rate of drug use may be linked to the country's social milieu or social environment in which people live, act, work, and age. Hawkins (1992) has expressed the view that contextual factors such as national laws, social norms, and drug availability, among other factors, are risk factors associated with initiation of drug use or changes in drug using behavior (like abuse) among adolescents. The UNODC 2018 report has similarly highlighted the role of macro-level environmental factors and mentioned that young people who experience extreme poverty or a lack of resources were subject to a host of environmental and health factors including homelessness, street involvement, exposure to toxic substances, and work at a young age.

Table 18. Regional Profile of Drugs Use Disorders: All age Groups, 2000-2016

Regions	2000 DUD DALYs (%)	2016 DUD DALYs (%)
AFR	6.7	9.6
AMR	10.36	19.9
EMR	10.95	15.06
EUR	13.1	14.4
SEAR	6.2	8.9
WPR	8.0	11.08
World	9.09	12.7

Source: Calculations using WHO Data from Global Disease Burden database

6.2 AGE DISTRIBUTION OF SUBSTANCE USE DISORDERS WITH SPECIAL FOCUS ON ADOLESCENTS AND YOUTH

The Global Burden of Disease study by Whiteford et al. (2013) found that while the burden of mental and substance use disorders spanned all age groups, the highest proportion of DALYs occurred in adolescents and young to middle-aged adults (aged 10–29 years). Among adolescents, alcohol has been the most commonly used psychoactive drug (Guo, Hawkins, Hill, & Abbott, 2001). Most research around the globe testifies that early (12–14 years old) to late (15–17 years old) adolescence is a critical risk period for the initiation of substance use and that substance use may peak among young people aged 18–25 years (UNODC 2018, booklet 4). According to the U.S. Addiction Center, drug abuse and mental disorders like depression and anxiety are commonly found together in teens. The abuse of alcohol and other psychoactive drugs during adolescence and early adulthood has become a serious public health issue in modern societies (Hawkins et al. 1992). As per WHO (2018) estimates, more than a quarter (26.5%) of all 15–19-year old worldwide are current drinkers. Prevalence rates of current drinking are highest among 15–19-year old in the WHO European Region (43.8%), followed by the Region of the Americas (38.2%) and the Western Pacific Region (37.9%) (WHO 2014). In case of U.S. adolescents, estimates over the period 2001 to 2004 indicated that alcohol misuse was common among adolescents. Slightly more than 40% of all 13–14-year-old adolescents in the United States report alcohol use and 10% of this age group exhibit regular use. These figures rose to almost 65% for any alcohol use reported and 27% for individuals who report regular use by age 16 (Whelan et al 2014).

Adolescence is a period of heightened vulnerability for engagement in addictive and risky behavior. Medical science attests that adolescence is the key period of development of SUDs, with striking increases across adolescence into early adulthood (Merikangas & McClair, 2012). Risk-taking and decision-making behaviors undergo development changes during adolescence (Balogh, Mayes, & Potenza, 2013). Disadvantageous decision-making and increased risk-taking may lead to increased vulnerability to addictions (Balogh et al (2013). There is consistent evidence that "youth who start drinking and heavy drinking at a younger age are at significantly greater risk for a range of alcohol problems, including car crashes, drinking and driving, suicidal thoughts and attempts, unintentional injury, as well as drug and alcohol dependence later in life" (Friese and Grube 2010 P5,). It is well documented that the risk of development of an AUD increases with the frequency of binge drinking (Connor et al 2016). Comorbid disorders can also be seen among youth, during the transition to young adulthood (age 18 to 25 years) (NIDA 2018). This coexistence of mental illness with drug or alcohol addiction is considered to be a menacing mental health problem. The combined effects act as a major global risk factor for disability and premature loss of life. Psychiatric disorders during early years in life are negatively correlated to emotional well-being, health, and education both in the short- and the long-term (Collishaw 2015 quoted by Choi OECD 2018). Evidence from countries shows that NEET youth faces a higher risk of propensity to substance abuse than other young people (Godfrey et al. 2002). A study (Benjet et al. 2012) of Mexican youth revealed that NEET youth were the prime targets of exploitation by organized drug peddlers' gangs.

Countries have taken steps to curb the prevalence of substance use among school and college students. In the United States, the survey by Monitoring the Future (MTF) in 2018, reveals a downward trend in the use of illicit drugs and heavy consumption of alcohol by the school students for grades 8, 10, and 12 since the peak period of 1997. This welcoming trend, however, is noticed along with a growing perverse perception among teenage populations, that they are seeing occasional drug use as less likely to be a problem or a risk (MTF 2018). This trend in attitudes towards drinking and drug use raises a scary specter that the usage rates might creep up in near future. More troubling results for the United States show that the age of onset of alcohol-use has been decreasing over the last 35 years, with youth now initiating drinking at just 12 years old on average, and the median age of onset of SUDs at around 15 years of age (Castellanos-Ryan et al 2013). The ESPAD report collects and monitors data about alcohol and drug use among 15 to 16 year-old students in European countries. Temporal trends over the last two decades (1995-2015) indicate an overall decrease in the prevalence rate of alcohol use in lifetime and last 30 days of use of alcohol from 89% to 81% and from 56% to 47%, respectively, but the trend of heavy episodic drinking (HED) has remained largely unchanged (The 2015 ESPAD report), showing a meager overall decline from 36% to 35%, among boys in the 20 year period. In the case of illicit drugs, the upward trend has remained largely unchanged in Europe (The 2015 ESPAD Report).

Disease Burden of Substance Use Disorder: Global and Regional Profile

A major proportion of the disease burden and deaths for young people in developed nations is attributable to misuse of alcohol and illicit drugs (Toumbourou et al 2007). In young men aged 20–24 years, alcohol and illicit substance use are responsible for 14% of total health burden at the global level (Degenhardt et al 2016). Globally, the burden from DUDs was greatest among young adults (ages 15–29 years) (Whiteford et al 2013). For AUDs, the largest burden occurred at between ages 25 and 50 years, followed by a gradual decline (Whiteford 2013). The following Table 19 provides evidence of growing DALYs per thousand of population relating to mental and drug use disorders at the global level. Data presented in Table 19 below pertain to three broad age groups: all ages, age group 15–29, and age group 30–49. As per the WHO's substance use report (2018), all HED prevalence rates among drinkers of 15–24 years are higher than in the total population, except for the Eastern Mediterranean Region. Estimates at the world level shows that prevalence of HED is lower among adolescents (15–19 years) than in the total population but it peaks at the age of 20–24 years when it becomes higher than in the total population (WHO 2018). Episodic drinking to the point of intoxication greatly increases the risks of accidents, injuries, violence and heart diseases (Connor et al 2016). Surveys on drug use among the general population consistently show that peak levels of drug use are seen among those aged 18–25, as well as the extent of drug use among young people, in particular past-year and past-month prevalence, which are indicators of recent and regular use, remains much higher than prevalence among older people (UNODC 2018, booklet 4).

Table 19. Labor Market Regulations and Prevalence of Mental and Substance-Use Disorders 2000–2016: DALYs Per Head of Population

Countries	Regulation on temporary forms of employment 2013	Prevalence of Mental and Substance abuse disorders 2015
Canada	0.21	18.95
USA	0.33	21.55
UK	0.54	17.6
New Zealand	0.92	18.4
Australia	1.04	21.62
Sweden	1.17	18.19
Netherlands	1.17	18.4
Norway	3.42	18.17
France	3.75	18.49
Slovak Republic	2.42	14.49
Poland	2.33	14.21
Slovenia	2.13	14.94
Czech Republic	2.13	14.57
World Average		15.47

Source: Calculations based upon WHO database on Disease Burden

As evident from Table 19, adolescents and young adult populations in the age group 15–29 had the highest DALY rate due to DUDs in both the years 2000 and 2016. This age group also experienced a relatively sharp increase in DALYs from mental disorders (net of substance use) during the same time period compared to other age groups mentioned above.

Tables 20 and 21 present regional variations in mental and substance use for 2000 and 2016.

Table 20. Mental and Substance-Use Disorders by Regions 2016: DALY Per Head of Population (in the 15–29 Age Group)

Regions	Mental Disorders (15-29) 2016	Alcohol Use Disorders (15-29) 2016	Drug Use Disorders (15-29) 2016
Africa	21	3	3
America	23	4	9
Europe	21	5	7
EMR	22	2	6
SEAR	18	2	3
WPR	18	2	4

Source: Calculations based upon WHO databases on disease burden

Table 21. Mental and Substance-Use Disorders by Regions 2000: DALY Per Head of Population (in the 15–29 Age Group)

Regions	Mental Disorders 2000	Alcohol Use Disorders 2000	Drug Use Disorders 2000
Africa	15.62	1.93	1.86
America	19.54	3.81	5.8
Europe	19.08	5.25	4.1
EMR	18.27	1.15	3.44
SEAR	16.81	1.85	1.83
WPR	17.4	1.83	2.4

Source: Calculations based upon WHO databases on disease burden

As shown in Table 22, mental and substance-abuse burden faced by youth (age group 15–29) has increased across all the world regions between 2000 and 2016. The youth in the region of the Americas is affected by the highest disease burden compared to all other regions. In a meta-analysis of socioeconomic status of substance use by adolescents, Lemstra et al (2008) found that adolescents with low socioeconomic status are 22% more likely to engage in marijuana and alcohol risk behavior than other adolescents with higher socioeconomic status.

Table 22. Proportion of Mental Disorder DALYs(in the age group 15-29) Attributable to Alcohol Use Disorders (AUD) and Drugs Use Disorders (DUD) : 2000-2016

Regions	2000 AUD DALYs(%)	2016 AUD DALYs	2000 DUD DALYs(%)	2016 DUD DALYs
AFR	10.2	10.9	11.7	12.7
AMR	12.1	11.5	21.1	25.6
EMR	5.1	5.6	18.3	19.1
EUR	15.3	14.1	23.5	20.5
WPR	8.0	8.4	17.3	16.1
World	10.0	9.66	17.11	17.38

Source: Calculations based upon WHO databases on disease burden

With the exception of high-income North America, and North Africa and the Middle East, the DALYs attributable to alcohol have been found to be higher than those attributable to drug use (See table 5 in GBD 2016, Alcohol and Drug use Collaborators) in 2016.

7. MENTAL AND SUBSTANCE-USE DISORDERS IN BRICS

In developing regions, demographic and epidemiological transitions are contributing to a rise in the absolute burden of mental, neurological, and substance-use disorders (Whiteford et al. 2016, Ch. 2). Despite this challenge, mental care services are less accessible to people due to shortage of resources, undeveloped institutions, and lack of legal protection mechanisms (e.g., viz., poorly equipped primary health sector, shortage of community resources, absences of pooled financing system at the national level, nonexistent research-based institutions, lack of universal coverage) in LMICs (Peters et al. 2008). Another formidable challenge is that these countries also suffer from a wide range of adverse structural conditions. These include viz., income and wealth inequalities, limited employment opportunities in the organized sector, widespread poverty, poor social support networks, high rates of illiteracy among rural populations, preponderance of unscientific beliefs (e.g., evil spirits), persistence of discrimination and human rights violations, stigma attached to mental illness, etc.

The data in Table 23 show that the prevalence of depressive mental disorders exceeded the world average of 4.4% in Russia, Brazil, South Africa, and India. In addition, the Brazilian population also has a high prevalence of anxiety disorders compared to other BRICS countries and the world average. Looking at the disease burden in terms of DALYs for all ages, we observe nearly similar extreme patterns with both Russia and Brazil showing quite a high disease burden from substance (alcohol and drugs combined) use compared to their peers in other BRICS countries. Degenhardt et al. (2013), in their study of illicit drug use, reported that Russia was among the countries (that include the United States, United Kingdom, and Australia) among the group of the highest rate of substance-use burden (>650 DALYs per 100,000 population). An empirical survey about Brazilian adolescent and older populations revealed that alcohol use was highly prevalent among adolescents, and exposure to domestic violence was positively associated with the use of tobacco and illegal substances. This study also observed a significant association of depression with alcohol abuse/dependence only.

Table 23. Prevalence of Depressive and Anxiety Disorders: Percent of Population, BRICS 2015

Countries/Regions	Depressive	Anxiety
Brazil	5.8	9.3
China	4.2	3.1
India	4.5	3
Russia	6.6	3.1
South Africa	4.6	3.4
World	4.4	3.6

Source: WHO 2017 Depression and Other Common Mental Disorders Global Health Estimates.

The following subsection deals with the health system resources and upstream structural determinants.

7.1 MENTAL HEALTH SYSTEM IN BRICS

Compared to the more developed OECD countries, the mental health sector in LMICs is under-resourced and underdeveloped. Mental health care is still not a priority in most LMICs (OECD 2016; Saxena et al. 2007). The following Table 24 provides comparison among different income group countries with respect to selected health indicators, such as resources (e.g., financial, skilled manpower, and hospital beds capacity) deployed in the provision of mental health services.

Table 24. Mental Health Resources among Developed and Developing Nations: Comparative View of Selected Indicators

Regions	Median Govt Health Expenditure per capita 2016 US $	Median Govt Expenditure On Hospitals per capita 2016 US $	Mental Health Workforce per 100,000 Pop 2017	Physiatrists per 100,000 2017	Total number of residential care bed per 100,000 2017
Low Income	0.02	0.02	1.6	0.1	
Lower Middle Income	1.05	0.53	6.2	0.5	
Upper Middle Income	2.62	2.25	20.6	2.1	2.0
High Income	80.24	35.06	71.7	12.7	23.3

Source: Mental Health ATLAS (WHO 2017).

We observe from Table 24, a wide gap between the resources available for meeting the health care needs between developed and developing countries. It is estimated that between 76% and 85% of people with severe mental disorders receive no treatment for their disorder in low-income and middle-income countries. The corresponding range for high-income countries is also high: between 35% and 50% (WHO 2013a).

As seen from above Table 24, the number of specialized and general health workers dealing with mental health in low-income and middle-income countries is grossly inadequate since half of the world's population resides in those regions. Community residential care facilities are nonexistent and negligible in most of the developing world, despite evidence-based support and recommendations from the WHO (2013a; Saxena et al. 2007). Most LMICs have underdeveloped primary health care systems, suffer from a lack of epidemiological data research, and lack integration of mental-health programs into general youth health and welfare programs (Patel et al. 2007). The integration of primary health care into hospital institutions is a suggested solution for the existing shortage of psychiatrists in these countries. Based on statistics regarding the mental health treatment gap in high-income countries as well as in LMICs, the Lancet Global Mental Health Group (2007) recommended a substantial increase in the overall volume of services provided to treat individuals with mental disorders in every country, in order to ensure that the available care is proportionate to the magnitude of need. In the authors' view, scaling up should encompass a basic, evidence-based package of services for core mental health disorders (Lancet Global Mental Health Group 2007).

Comparison among BRICS

Table 25 provides a comparative picture of BRICS countries in terms of available mental health resources. China and India particularly are facing ominous challenges of a low level of public spending, inadequate numbers of skilled human resources and hospital beds (including community residential beds per 100,000 population). The country profile provided in "Mental Health Atlas" (country profile, 2011, 2014, WHO) shows that these two countries along with South Africa do not keep sufficient records and information on vital mental health activities and services rendered from the mental and community institutions. The integration of the primary care sector into hospital services remained weak especially in India due to a lack of trained manpower (Van Gineken et al. 2014). China has to go a long way to meet the target of providing mental health care in the community (Liu et al. 2011).

Patel et al. (2016) analyzed the magnitude of the treatment gap in the mental health of youth in India and China and found that human and financial resources for mental health were grossly inadequate, with less than 1% of the national health care budget allocated to mental health in either country. These authors commenting on the delivery of mental health services in these countries remarked that poor quality of care and violations of human rights, involuntary admittance to an institution, abandonment by family members, restrictions and isolation, and inadequate living conditions, were longstanding concerns in mental hospitals in both China and India. Comparing financing patterns in India and China, Patel et al. (2016) found that the public sector in China was the major provider of mental health care, and 86% of the psychiatric beds and close to 70% of all health facilities that provided mental health care were directly funded by the government. In contrast, India's largest service provider was the rapidly growing and mostly unregulated private sector.

Evidence suggests that in the absence of adequate public funding support, certain socially disadvantaged groups tend to use health services less, although these groups may need health services more. This phenomenon, sometimes referred to as "inverse care law," can partly be explained by the fact that disadvantaged groups typically face multiple barriers in accessing services (OECD 2016; Peters et al. 2008). These include financial barriers, such as direct and indirect costs of accessing services as well as geographic and sociocultural barriers (OECD 2016). It is estimated that only 2% of people with mental disorders in LMICs—where 85% of the world's population lives—receive treatment (Eaten et al. 2011). Out-of-pocket (OOP) spending is the dominant mode of financing the health care needs among the population in most developing countries. Numerous studies have shown that OOP payment is an inequitable and inefficient way of mobilizing resources for health services (WHO 2005). Among BRICS, the OOP burden is highest in India.

Both South Africa and Brazil show a high percentage of government spending (% of GDP) on health. South Africa has relatively the lowest burden of OOP expenditure compared to the other BRICS countries (Table 25). In South Africa, the treatment gap is quite low, which may reflect its greater spending (8.6% of GDP) on health care in comparison with other LMICs, and even some high-income countries (Wang et al. 2008).

The availability of qualified human resources is essential to addressing mental health issues adequately, and in that respect, great disparities among BRICS are observed. Brazil and Russia have greater densities of psychiatrists and nurses per 100,000 inhabitants (Buss, Ferreira, and Hoirisch 2014). However, in Russia, care remains predominantly institution-based, and community-based treatment and care facilities are limited (Jenkins et al. 2007). Community-based facilities and integration of primary care into the mental health institutions are being considered as priority areas for future expansion (Shek et al. 2010). In Brazil, the CAPS(Community Psychosocial Centers) system became the cornerstone of the Brazilian Psychiatric Reform.

Table 25. Selected Indicators of Mental Health Resources (2011) in BRICS

Country	Beds (Mental Hos) Per 100,000	Beds in community residential beds per 100,000	Number of Community Residential facilities, per 100,000	Psychiatrists/ Nurses Per 100,000	Government expenditure on health % GDP/ Mental health spending per capita US $
Brazil	18.1	2.31	0.29	3.07/ 1.6	9.05/43.1
China	13.7	UN	UN	1.53/2.6	4.55
India	1.46	UN	UN	0301/0.166	4.16
Russia	109	0.25	0.01	11.61/46	5.44/10.2
South Africa	19.5	3.47	0.12	0.27/9.72	8.51

Source: Mental Health Atlas: Country Profile 2011 and Mental Health Atlas 2014. Notes: UN refers to unavailable

These CAPS units provide community services responsible for treating severe mental disorders and to articulate the liaison with primary care units to coordinate psychiatric care in a defined catchment area (Mateus et al. 2008). Another innovative services program, called the "Return Home program" is seen in Brazil and to some extent South Africa, where they have more developed community-based facilities to supplement delivery of mental health services. Information available from the Mental Health Atlas (2011) shows that among BRICS, Brazil and to some extent Russia use a system of information management for mental health activities.

7.2 SOCIAL AND ECONOMIC FACTORS AND MENTAL DISORDERS IN BRICS

To deal with mental health issues, the World Mental Health Report (Desjarlais et al. 1995) emphasized the need for broadening the scope and context of mental health beyond its traditional biomedical boundaries, to include the larger social determinants and consequences of mental illness (Patel 2007; Viner et al. 2012). Socioeconomic barriers to economic growth, mass poverty, and wide disparities in accessing essential resources have been identified as factors leading to unmet needs for mental health services in most underdeveloped countries. The rapid growth of BRICS has been accompanied by adverse developments of uneven income and wealth distribution in these countries. As shown in Table 26, compared to the OECD average of 5.1, the quintile ratios in South Africa, China, India, and Brazil are significantly higher, indicating a much wider gap between the top and bottom 20%. The OECD report (2010) that analyzed income inequality trends in BRICS from 1993 to 2008, reported that the fall in poverty rates in BRICS accompanied a significant fall in inequality only in Brazil, mainly due to the progressive resurgence of the middle class. Inequality levels in China and India are lower among BRICS, but still exceed OECD average levels. Evidence indicates that the BRCIS labor markets are characterized by a higher degree of informality than the OECD countries which affects the less privileged more significantly and contributes to the persistence of income inequalities (OECD 2010). Wealth inequality is found to be the highest in the Russian Federation, followed by India among BRICS countries. Wealth inequality is more acute among BRICS countries than most of the OECD countries (compare Tables 12 and 22).

The youth poverty rate is highest in South Africa, and China ranks second (Table 26). Youth poverty rates in these countries exceeds the OECD average of 14%. Estimates show that of the 20% of adolescents and youth across the globe who experience a mental health condition each year, those living in low-income countries make up 85–90% of this group. Estimates for the Asia Pacific region, which contains 60% of the world's youth population, indicate that young people face numerous barriers that result in exclusion, from lacking access to quality education and decent jobs to a scarcity of youth-friendly health care services (UN ESCAP 2014).

Table 26. Social Economic Factors of Health Inequity

Countries	Gini Coefficient 2016	Quintile Ratio 2016	Youth Poverty Rate (Relative Threshold) (Latest Available)	Wealth Inequality 2016	Percentage Health Care Expenditure not financed by Private OOP(ILO) 2011
India	0.495	13.3	15.6	87.6	40.6
China	0.514	28.15	22	81.9	65.2
Russian Federation	0.376	7.1	13.8	92.3	64.6
South Africa	0.623	41.25	29.5	83	92.8
Brazil	0.470	12.4	18	82.9	68.7

Source: OECD Databases.

7.3 SUBSTANCE USE AMONG YOUTH IN BRICS

While the developed countries have been struggling to stabilize substance use for decades, many developing countries and countries with former socialist economies are also experiencing a rising tide of alcohol use (including early onset and excessive drinking), cigarette smoking, and use of illicit drugs. Major increases in injection drug use, which carries the highest health risks, are recorded. Opiate injecting in eastern European countries and south and Southeast Asia and use of amphetamine in many regions (WHO 2004c) continue to rise. It was estimated that almost half of all people who inject drugs (PWID) worldwide, in 2016, lived in just three countries: China, the Russian Federation, and the United States. Although these three countries combined account for just 27% of the global population aged 15–64 years, together they are home to 45% of the world's PWID (UNODC 2018). According to the cannabis use perception index, the increase in cannabis use over the period of 2010 to 2016 appeared to have been greatest in countries in Asia and Africa, followed by increases in countries in the Americas and Europe (UNODOC 2018). AUDs have been found to be most prominent in Brazilian and U.S. women (Rehm et al. 2009).

As mentioned in several studies and above, young people start to use substances, singly or in combination, at early ages, and this is becoming a worldwide epidemic (Gruskin, Plafker, and Smith-Estelle 2001). Comparing Tables 27 and 28, the burden of DUDs (in DALYs) in the age group 15–29 is much higher across all BRICS in comparison to the all-age group category. Among these countries, Russians have the highest burden of drug and alcohol-use disorders among youth (15–29 age group) and all-age group categories.

Table 27. Mental and Substance-Use Disorders (BRICS) 2016: DALY (000) Per Head of Population

Regions	Mental Disorders (Per 000, All Ages)	Alcohol use Disorders (per 000, All Ages)	Drug Use Disorders (per 000, All Ages)
Brazil 2016	21	5.53	2.58
China 2016	17.68	1.85	2.50
India 2016	17.24	1.96	1.91
Russia 2016	17.44	14.31	9.28
South Africa 2016	16.84	2.34	2.58

Source: Calculations based on WHO databases on the disease burden

Table 28. Mental and Substance-Use Disorders (BRICS) 2016: DALY (000) Per Head of Population (The 15–29 Age Group)

Regions	Mental Disorders	Alcohol Use Disorders	Drug Use Disorders
Brazil 2016	23.78	5.06	4.75
China 2016	17.38	1.85	3.76
India 2016	18.44	1.88	2.98
Russia 2016	19	11.18	14.56
South Africa 2016	22.26	3.20	4.24

Source: Calculations based on WHO databases on the disease burden

The following subsection traces the problem of substance abuse in Russia.

7.4 CHALLENGE OF SUBSTANCE ABUSE IN RUSSIAN REPUBLIC

The Russian Republic faces an alarmingly high and unabated burden (years lost due to premature deaths and disability) of substance abuse among its population. In Russia, heavy drinking has a long tradition and the historical evidence reveals, to a considerable extent, this culture has been created by successive governments, whether Czarist or Communist. The history of alcohol consumption in Russia shows that, at various times, the state has contributed substantially to the problem, through the production and distribution of cheap alcohol (McKee 1999). Further, studies corroborate that alcoholism increases the likelihood of developing co-occurring conditions such as SUDs. A person who abuses alcohol has a greater risk of using at least one other sub- stance, such as marijuana, cocaine, or heroin. Prolonged consumption of drugs and alcohol increases the user's tolerance thus requiring more of the substance to achieve the same desirable effects. Examining the comorbidity between DSM-IV alcohol and specific drug use disorders in the United States, Stinson et al.

(2005) found that prevalence was 7.35% for alcohol use disorders only, 0.90% for drug use disorder only, and 1.10% for comorbid alcohol and drug use disorders. Russia, by virtue of its geographical location, is both a transshipment and a destination country for Afghanistan's opiates. The trafficking in opium and heroin from Afghanistan through the Central Asian states remains the main cause of drug availability in Russia. This availability has been exploited by an increase in the number of people with low-level incomes (students, jobless youth in the cities, and unemployed workers in small towns and rural areas, conscripts, etc.) in "street level" drug trafficking in the country with the passage of time.

Among the best practices and strategies, it has been suggested to adopt a public health approach for drug laws and policies to prevent, reduce, and respond to the potential harms of drugs while respecting human rights and promoting health and well-being(Toronto Public Health 2018).

8. PUBLIC HEALTH POLICY: EVIDENCE BASED PREVENTIVE INTERVENTIONS

Given the far-reaching economic and social consequences of mental disorders, it is essential that greater attention be given to prevention and promotion in mental health at the level of policy formulation, legislation, decision-making, resource allocation, and the overall health care system (WHO 2002; White ford et al. 2013). The task in preventive interventions is to decrease risk and/or increase protection in the individual, the family environment, and the wider environment with which the individual comes into contact (Institute of Medicine [US], 1994). Gordon (1983) has proposed the definition of prevention as measures adopted by or practiced on persons not currently feeling the effects of a disease, intended to decrease the risk that disease will afflict them in the future. Mental health promotion, on the other hand, aims to enhance an individual's ability to achieve psychosocial well-being and cope with adversity (Kalra et al. 2012). In nutshell, prevention is concerned with avoiding disease (WHO 2002), while the promotion programs aim to develop important competencies to promote wellness (Durlac and Wells 1997). In mental health promotion programs, the central idea is that mental health is more than the absence of mental illness (Keyes 2007). These policies complement each other, as both of them involve associated activities that improve the overall quality of life for people and their society. For instance, public interventions that aim to reduce risk factors predisposing children and adults to mental disorders, and programs that strengthen the protective factors reinforce the effects of each other.

Biological and neurological sciences, along with social epidemiology research studies have provided substantial insight into the role of risk and protective factors in the developmental pathways to mental disorders and poor mental health (WHO 2004a). Evidence on multiple determinants of mental health call for public health policy that extend its reach beyond the health sector, seeking improvements across a wide range of social and economic determinants that make people ill in the first place (Wilkinson and Marmot 2003). The discussion below draws upon the studies of a widely employed prevention framework.

The WHO report on prevention (2002) classifies primary prevention further into three categories: (i) universal prevention policies that target the general public or a whole population group, (ii) selective prevention policies that target individuals or subgroups of the population whose risk of developing a mental disorder is significantly higher than that of the rest of the population, and (iii) indicated prevention-that is targeting persons at high risk for mental disorders. The following Table 29 lists the constituents of these prevention programs in a generic form.

Table 29. Primary-Level Prevention Policies and Their Focus

Types of Primary Interventions	Selected Elements and Focus
(i)**Universal prevention policies**	Life course approach of prevention and health promotion (covering all stages human development throughout the life span) (Institute of medicine, US 1994); social and nutritional support, home visiting programs beginning at preconception and pre-natal period (WHO 2004a); strengthening of early childhood development programs (Shonkoff et al 2012, WHO 2014a); school-based programs that help children negotiate stressful transition (Durlak and Wells 1997); resilience developing curriculum in schools; strengthening of primary health care services with trained primary physician and health care staff in mental health (Durlak and Wells 1997) to facilitate early detection; thrust on inclusive growth strategy that reduce income disparities, improve housing conditions, provide enhanced opportunities of access to higher education and training;

(ii) *Selective prevention* policies that target individuals or subgroups of the population whose risk of developing a mental disorder is significantly higher than that of the rest of the population	Developing epidemiological database; programs targeting children of alcoholic parents or those from low-income single-parent families (or about to divorce families) (Durlak and Wells 1997); monitoring the school environment to curtail social bullying instances; paying special attention to those at the risk of drop-outs; designing policies of proportionate universalism, (universal and targeted policy framework; Carey et al 2015); collaborative care model, with treatment facilities in primary health care setting to overcome social 'stigma' problem; special programs for people and families in war affected areas (Seal et al 2007)
(iii) *Indicated preventive interventions* aim at mental health programs for children and adolescents that seek to identify early signs of maladjustment and to intervene before full-blown disorders develop (Durlak and Miles 1998). These authors term these as secondary interventions.	Screen of child and adolescent populations, targeting cases of early onset of mental disorders; expanded roles for service providers (e.g. collaborative mental care facilities) in addition to traditional forms of therapy for established problems; intervention using cognitive-behavior or behavioral techniques; psychotherapy for children with established problems (Durlak and Wells 1998)

8.2 UNIVERSAL PREVENTION POLICIES

The accumulated research evidence overwhelmingly indicates that no credible outcomes can be achieved by lop-sided strategies that narrowly focus on treating the symptoms of mental illness. Evidence shows that most resources are being devoted to treat disease and relatively few to modifying the predisposing factors (Adler and Newman 2002). Countries cannot promote national mental health only by reducing mental illness (Keyes 2007). The determinants of health are multiple, and include factors such as income, social support, early childhood development, education, employment, housing, and gender (WHO 2003; Wilkinson and Marmot eds.). In a universal strategy (also called a global or population-wide approach), all members in an available population receive the intervention (Durlak and

Wells 1997).

The WHO report (2014a) on social determinants of mental health has proposed a wide ranging role of the public policy, embracing a life- course approach (from prenatal, early childhood period to older ages) as well as measures that address all social domains of life. These include family relationships, neighborhood conditions, community resources, and country-level structural factors (such as unemployment, and the level [generosity] of social welfare) as important factors in the causal pathway to health.

Legal and supply restrictions influence the availability during prescribed hours and to eligible population, as well as price level-both meant to limit consumption. Availability and social acceptability exert powerful influence that increases the likelihood of drug use.

Most mental disorders begin during the adolescence and early youth period (12–24 years of age), although they are often first detected later in life (Patel et al. 2007). As a result, interventions that focus on children and young adults and detect onset at early or beginning stage are considered to be highly effective (Kessler et al. 2005).

Preconception and the prenatal period are significant both for the mother and for her child. Studies suggest that fetal exposure to maternal stress can influence later stress responsiveness (Shonkoff et al. 2012). When developing biological systems are strengthened by positive early experiences, children are more likely to thrive and grow up to be healthy, contributing adults. Sound health in early childhood provides a foundation for the construction of sturdy brain architecture and the achievement of a broad range of skills and learning capacities (Shonkoff et al. 2012). Taking action to improve the conditions of daily life from before birth, during early childhood, at school age, during family building and working ages, and at older ages provides opportunities both to improve population mental health and to reduce the risk of those mental disorders that are associated with social inequalities (WHO 2014).

To protect against potential risks during the period of infancy and early childhood, studies suggest the critical role of protective interventions like public health, social support programs, early childhood development programs, community counseling, and parenting education and training, to mention only a few of them.

Universal school-based violence prevention programs represent an important means of reducing violent and aggressive behavior as suggested by Hahn et al. (2007) in their study about the United States. The findings by Durlak et al. (2011) from a meta-analysis of school-based, universal social and emotional learning (SEL) programs involving pupils from kindergarten through high school, support the growing body empirical evidence regarding the positive impact of SEL programs on improving social and emotional skills, attitudes, and behavior.

Population-based macro-level strategies that deal with policies of economic and social development need to address structural determinants of mental health such as programs that reduce poverty, discrimination, and inequalities, and promote access to education, meaningful employment, and housing problems. The chain of events leading to an adverse health outcome includes both proximal and distal causes— proximal factors act directly or almost directly to cause disease, and distal causes are further back in the causal chain and act via several intermediary causes (WHO 2002). While safe and supportive families and schools, together with positive and supportive peers are crucial to mental health, Viner et al. (2012), in their study, found strongest support favoring structural determinants of health, such as national wealth, income inequality, and access to education. Inequalities (e.g, within education and wealth) and inadequate employment among young adults have been found as great risk factors to mental health.

The structural impediments, as discussed above, are the result of poor development strategies and policies at the national level. The non-inclusive growth path has created unequal opportunities for advancement that resulted in the social exclusion of people with limited access to resources.

Inclusive Growth Policies and Mental Health

Over past decade, declining productivity and growing inequalities worldwide have undermined the potential of steady and stable growth. Interrupted growth periods have led countries to resort to fiscal consolidation measures from time to time to keep the public debt under control. In practice, fiscal consolidation episodes have (a) widened income inequalities, (b) led to a significant and long-lasting fall in the wage income share, and (c) raised long-term unemployment in OECD countries (Ball et al. 2014). Inequality harms the economy through different channels: (a) weak aggregate demand (Dabla-Norris et al. 2015; OECD 2016; Stiglitz 2016), (b) inequality of opportunity (Stiglitz 2016), (c) less public investment in productive areas, like infrastructure, technology, and education (Cingano 2014; Stiglitz 2016), (d) depriving the ability of lower income households to stay healthy, and (e) lowering the opportunities of mobility between generations (Corak 2013). Due to the twin challenges of slow productivity growth and widening inequalities, the economies have come under the grip of "secular stagnation" (Gordon 2015; Summers 2015). The prolonged period of stagnating living standards and fiscal consolidation have adversely affected the economic futures of large shares of the youth population in many countries.

Recognizing the adverse impact of income disparities and weak aggregate demand, researchers have started advocating inclusive economic development strategies for promoting economic prosperity with equity of outcomes. Inclusive growth is growth that not only creates new economic opportunities, but also ensures equal access to the opportunities it creates for all segments of society, including the disadvantaged and the marginalized (Ali 2007). The strategy of inclusive growth envisages the path of development over the entire life cycle of people, starting from the population-based measures necessary to respond to early childhood development (ECD) needs, to enhance the quality of education, to reduce educational failure in elementary and high schools, to enrich the quality of neighborhood and community environment, to provide youth with opportunities of vocational education, and to motivate youth to engage in pro-social activities. The inclusive growth approach takes a longer-term perspective, as the focus is on productive employment rather than on direct income redistribution, as a means of increasing incomes for excluded groups (Commission on Growth and Development 2008). Public policies that make substantial new investments in education and training to enable youth to update and maintain their skills, and to provide opportunities for careers and upward mobility are necessary (Cingano 2014; Kalleberg 2009a) for durable growth with shared prosperity in the economy.

8.2 SELECTED INTERVENTION POLICIES

Under this set of policies, groups considered at risk for eventual problems, but who are not yet dysfunctional, are targeted for intervention (Durlac and Wells 1997). To operationalize selective intervention policies for prevention, it is important that countries have epidemiological databases that provide information on how often a problem occurs, where it occurs, and how many people it affects over time. The data need to be collected on a regular basis on the incidence of illness across the life-course, from childhood into adolescence and emerging adult- hood, and related associated possible precursors and biomarkers. Epidemiological evidence on illness can serve as a useful base for designing prevention policies and determining the allocation of resources.

One of the cornerstones of targeted prevention policy is early detection interventions. This approach can be termed as a prospective approach, since it contributes to the objective of determining the earliest deviations from health (i.e., providing very early detection of disease onset) so as to intervene at the earliest stage and restore health rather than wait to manage chronic illness (Keyes 2007). There is a social gradient in mental health risks faced by people at different levels of social economic status. Most people below the median level of income have low education status and live in poor and congested neighborhoods. Children living with economically poor parents or disturbed and violent families face greater risk of neglect, poor nutrition, and lack of connectedness with school, education, and community. Additionally, many innocent children in school become victims of social bullying or fall victim to deviant peers. Shonkoff et al. (2009) state that the major risk factors for toxic stress include extreme poverty, recurrent physical and/ or emotional abuse, chronic neglect, severe maternal depression, parental substance abuse, and family violence. Such disadvantaged sections of people, and those with single parents and living in poor neighborhoods need greater, special, and targeted attention under public policy to escape social exclusion. Marmot et al. (2010) have termed such policies as public policy of proportionate universalism (scale and intensity that is proportionate to the level of disadvantage) aimed at ensuring a good start to life for every child (Marmot et al. 2012). Carey et al. (2015), however, add that in practice, proportionate universalism must com- bine a degree of "selectivity" within a universal framework, otherwise it will fail to flatten the social gradient.

Specific interventions to increase resilience in children and adolescents through parenting and early interventions, and programs for children at risk for mental disorders, such as those who have a mentally ill parent or have suffered parental loss or family disruption, have also shown to increase mental well-being and decrease depressive symptoms and the onset of depressive disorders. It is now well documented that government support policies and investment into ECD can play a vital role in providing equitable access to strong nurturing environments for all children (Irwin et al. 2007). ECD services provide the largest share of human contact with children, and are a source of social capital, such as parenting skills and family education (Irwin et al. 2007). Durlak and Wells (1997), in their review of 177 primary prevention programs found evidence that programs modifying the school environment, individually focused mental health promotion efforts, and attempts to help children negotiate stressful transitions yield significant mean effects ranging from 0.24 to 0.93.

8.3 INDICATIVE PREVENTION INTERVENTIONS

Indicative prevention policies aim to target those groups about to experience potentially stressful life events or transitions (Durlak and

Wells 1997). The Institute of Medicine (1994) suggested the term, "indicated preventive intervention," (or indicated prevention) be used instead of secondary prevention. Secondary prevention assumes a population perspective, as a particular population is screened or evaluated in some fashion (Durlak and Wells 1998). Indicated prevention targets of high risk are considered to have detectable signs or symptoms foreshadowing mental disorder or biological markers indicating predisposition for mental disorder, but they do not meet diagnostic criteria for disorder at that time (Saxena et al. 2006, p. 6).

Research evidence suggests that effectiveness of prevention policies, particularly related to selective and indicative interventions, would depend to a great extent on the way the medical services are organized and delivered. The collaborative care model, integrating primary health services with the hospital-specialized psychiatric services, can deliver more cost-effective and timely care than in the traditional institutionalized facilities. In all countries, primary care and physicians are the first point of contact for patients. Therefore, trained primary care physicians (with additional training in mental health) working in collaboration with psychiatrists, hospital staff, and community workers would be able to render timely detection and preventive services in, without invoking the feeling of social stigma, which is generally attached to treatment sought in psychiatric institutions.

9. SUMMARY AND RECOMMENDATIONS

Mental disorders are among the most prevalent, chronic, and disabling health conditions; they touch the lives of people of all ages. The health, social, and economic consequences of poor mental health are substantial; yet, in most cases preventable. The prevalence of mild-to-moderate mental health disorders among young people in OECD countries and LMICs is becoming cause for serious concern. Global estimates reveal that approximately 20% of adolescents and youth experience a mental health condition—such as depression, anxiety disorders, and disruptive behavioral disorders—each year, and those living in low-income countries make up 85–90% of this group. People with mental illness often have physical comorbidities and higher mortality rates than the general population. Countries are often struggling to remove barriers (economic and social) and to adopt evidence-based practices in order to minimize the adverse consequences related to personal suffering, social risks, and economic costs.

Risks to health do not occur in isolation. Individuals and groups exist within a social context: the values and structure of their society (Hawkins et al. 1992). Risk factors need "contextualizing"[27]—that is, attempting to understand how people come to be exposed to individually based risk factors and to determine the social conditions under which individual risk factors (proximal causes) are related to disease (Link and Phelon 1995). Social determinants can be proximal and structural (or, distal) factors. Proximal factors act directly or almost directly to cause disease, and structural causes are further back in the causal chain and act via a number of intermediary causes. Evidence shows that the strongest determinants of health worldwide are structural factors such as national wealth, income inequality, and access to education (Viner et al. 2012). The distribution of economic and social resources explains health and other outcomes in the vast majority of studies (Friedli 2009). Thus, programs and policies addressing structural factors at the macro- and meso-levels offer an effective way to address mental and behavioral disorders. There is wide variation among OECD with the prevalence of mental and behavioral disorders. The present study uses cross data from OECD countries to attempt to identify the critical structural determinants that explain the variations across countries.

The study uses a PLSR approach to estimate the relative importance of the above-mentioned structural determinants. The variables of importance found in our empirical exercise were wealth distribution, quintile ratio, youth poverty, housing cost (rent) burden on the bottom quintile, employment protection level, and percentage of children in single-parent household. These results are consistent with existing empirical findings and theoretical predictive models that conditions of high economic-social inequalities, insecurity of employment, stressful work conditions, gender discrimination, poor parenting styles, bullying at school and workplaces, unhealthy lifestyles, poor housing conditions, and widespread human rights violations are among the decisive risk factors that warrant collective action and shared values in a society (WHO 2004d). While our cross-sectional study precluded interpretations of causality or directionality, there was enough existence of research evidence on the causal role of social determinants on mental health. Poor mental health is both a cause and a consequence of the experience of social, economic, and environmental inequalities (Friedli 2009). Our findings suggest that priority focus of ameliorative social programs and policies ought to be on the following determinants.

First, employment and working conditions merit the foremost priority of attention, since they contribute to health disparities through policy failures and psychosocial mechanisms suffered by people in precarious and low-paid jobs. The precariousness of employment can reflect social exclusion because it emphasizes both distributional (the lack of resources at the disposal of an individual or household) and relational aspects (the lack of social ties to the family, friends, local com- munity, state services and institutions or more generally to the society to which an individual belongs, and lack of power; Bhalla and Lapeyre 2004). Social exclusion exacerbates existing cleavages between groups and creates new ones. In the last few decades, there has been a steady decline in union membership and the weakening of workers' bargaining power and influence in most industrialized countries (Kalleberg 2009; Stiglitz 2016). In most OECD countries, data show that new entrants to the labor market are caught in a series of precarious jobs interspersed by relatively short periods of unemployment or economic inactivity (OECD 2010a). Active labor market policies and greater attention to human capital investments achieve both efficiency and equity in the labor market simultaneously (Ostry, Berg, and Tsangarides 2014).

For people with mental health problems, finding work in the open labor market or returning to work and retaining a job after treatment is often a challenge. Most people with a history of mental illness want to work, are perfectly capable of working in appropriate settings, and derive therapeutic benefits from working. However, those people often face barriers of reduced abilities because of their symptoms (even if only temporarily), endemic social stigma, and widespread discrimination by employers. Important barriers to employment such as stigma and discrimination must be overcome (Funk, Drew, and Knapp 2012; McDaid, Knapp, and Raja 2008; Mitchell and Harrison 2001; Thornicroft 2006; Thornicroft and Tansella 2009). Societies need to invest in supportive networks and institutions (Marmot 1999).

Second, it is important to address the growing and extreme inequalities in income and wealth. Growing inequalities retard long-term growth by dampening the growth of aggregate demand and diverting public investment from productive areas. The World Bank (2006) found a clear potential nexus: inequalities in income, wealth, or power translated into unequal opportunities and lead to wasted productive potential and inefficient allocation of resources. Slow economic growth and declining income share of the bottom quintile trigger a vicious spiral of weak aggregate demand, low productive investment, slow job creation, and increasing household debt. Policies of wage moderation, fiscal austerity, and easing of labor market regulations further exacerbate the gap between the rich and poor.

Third, increasing attention needs to be given to assist family responsibilities for promoting children's well-being. Falling marriage rates, increasing divorce rates, and lone parents are becoming the norms in the society. Family background (family wealth and social capital) play a dominant role in structuring a child's economic opportunities and earnings in life. It is suggested that interventions that increase the share of children who grow up with both parents could improve the overall well-being of children, albeit modestly (Amato 2005). Public-funded childcare support and special benefit programs can be offered.

Fourth, public housing programs of affordable housing units, flexible support services, and hygienic living surroundings are a vital necessity for ameliorating the risk of common mental disorders in adults (Lund et al. 2018). In most countries, there is a critical shortage of supporting housing units and the task of providing support services to individuals with serious mental illness has become a serious challenge. Even the challenges of providing basic shower facilities and meeting human hygienic needs of the homeless and sick people remains a significant barrier to self-care and personal cleanliness (Leibler et al. 2017). Past records of most countries bear testimony to the fact that provision of affordable housing remains a "tall promise." Countries even failed to meet the dire need of providing basic human living conditions to destitute, homeless, and mentally sick people in their recovery process.

Fifth, studies underscored the need for better data collection to obtain a complete assessment of mental health performance and shortfalls, including estimates on available resources for the treatment and magnitude of neuropsychiatric disorders, and standards of mental health quality services available to meet the health care needs. An effective surveillance system that provides ongoing comprehensive and timely information on the entire spectrum of the mental health population is necessary (Reeves et al. 2011).

Sixth, countries need to scale up efforts toward forging systematic integration of mental health services into primary health care to deliver cost-effective services for treatment of mild-to-moderate mental disorders. For other disorders, treatment in a community care setting ("community psychiatry") is proposed especially for treating major psychiatric illnesses, particularly the schizophrenias and the affective disorders (Goldberg and Huxley 1980). It is a setting in which the primary care system plays a central role in the detection and management of mental illness in the community. The underlying idea of this collaborative care model acknowledges that serious mental disorders require a long-term and systematic-recovery-based (rehabilitative) approach in community-based settings that puts the emphasis on supporting individuals with mental disorders and psychosocial disabilities to achieve aspirations and goals (Goodrich et al. 2013; Thornicroft et al. 2016; WHO 2014).

Seventh, frequent episodes of political violence, large-scale wars, and growing cases of institutional betrayals warrant serious attention and concerted efforts. Millions of people around the world are exposed to preventable traumatizing events such as child abuse, gun violence, sexual assaults, war, and torture (WHO 2004). Armed violence and political tensions in the Eastern Mediterranean region has wrought higher rates of age-standardized mental disorder DALYs compared to the global level (GBD 2015).

Institutional failures and betrayal cause traumatic and psychological distress (Smith 2016) to children and people.[28] Institutional betrayal can occur within families, governments and the military, organizations, work-places, religious institutions, medical clinics/hospitals, or any organizational system in which people are dependent on systemic protection (Freyd and Birrell 2013). Both exposure prevention and reduction of its duration can be realized by public measures such as preventing exposure to violence or abuse enhancing early detection (WHO 2004).

Finally, research studies have substantiated a firm connection between mental illness and the use of addictive substances. Longitudinal studies show that youth under 18 years of age are at high risk for developing substance use disorders in adolescence and adulthood (Salvo et al. 2012). Adolescence is universally a time of vulnerability to different influences because of the tendency to initiate various behaviors, which may include substance use (UNDOC 2018). Due to the comorbidity of substance abuse and mental disorders, it is suggested that mental disorders must be addressed as a central part of substance-abuse prevention efforts in every country (Regier et al. 1990). Evidence-based prevention and early intervention strategies are required to reduce the prevalence of substance-use practices among adolescents and youth. Studies under- scored that NEET youth were at heightened risk of substance abuse and juvenile crime indulgence (Baggio et al. 2015; Benjet et al. 2012; O'Dea et al. 2014; Yates and Payne 2007). Poverty and a lack of opportunities for social and economic advancement can lead young people to become involved in the drug-supply chain (UNODC 2018). These adverse trends and developments are taking place at a juncture when the world is facing an unprecedented challenge of responding to growing age dependency in near future.

Despite the wide recognition of the famous statement that "without mental health, there can be no true physical health,"[29] evidence, on the contrary, shows that countries have yet to respond effectively to ameliorate the long-standing socioeconomic barriers to the mental well-being of the population. Youth mental health matters in all countries, since it affects all sectors of society (Patel et al. 2007). Since the mid-1970s, there has been an erosion of workers' employment and working conditions (Benach et al. 2014). Millennial's job struggle is resulting in delayed adulthood. Arnett (2000) has argued that the adolescence period had lengthened as the age of marriage, parenthood, and school leaving had increased.

According to the European Commission's research report (Lodovici and Semenza 2012), the increasing diffusion of precarious jobs among young people, including highly educated ones, represents a social cost and extends the poverty risks and the income inequalities within and between generations. Poverty rates among NEET youth pose a special challenge and substantial cost for many countries. Improving employment and social integration among youth has become a prime policy concern (Carcillo et al. 2015).

Youth is finding itself at the crossroad to achieve work and life balance. Among the fiscal austerity measures undertaken in the spate of the economic slowdown (Summers 2015, 2016), social expenditure cuts are adding to the woes of struggling youth. At this critical time, some state and federal governments initiated the move of legalizing cannabis use and sale with a view to inject revenue into the tax coffers. This purported revenue gain needs to be weighed against social costs of such a move. Mental disorders have become the core health challenge of the twenty-first century (Wittchen et al. 2011). Evidence vehemently indicates that ultimately no durable progress can be attained unless we effectively tackle the causes of and the conditions in which people are born, grow, live, work, and age (WHO 2013d). Comprehensive strategies at the population level to address these social determinants are likely to improve mental health in the population and reduce inequities, because such strategies focus on improving the conditions in which people are born, grow live, work, and age (WHO 2014a).W

The most critical stage is the early childhood stage,[30] since the biology of early childhood adversity reveals that toxic stress (arising from risk factors such as extreme poverty, recurrent physical and/or emotional abuse, chronic neglect, severe maternal depression, parental substance abuse, and family violence) in young children can lead to less outwardly visible yet permanent changes in brain structure and function (Shonkoff and Garner 2012). In the near foreseeable future, transdisciplinary bridges between genetics, neuroscience, social sciences, psychiatry and the other mental health professions can collectively teach how to prevent and control mental disorders in the population to better improve overall mental health (Anthony 2005, Ch. 10 in Herman H et al. eds.).

REFERENCES

Aassve, A., Davia, M., Iacovou, M., & Mencarini, L. (2005) Poverty and the Transition to Adulthood: Risky Situations and Risky Events. Working Paper of Institute for Social and Economic Research.

Abdi, H. (2007). Partial least squares regression: PLS regression. In N. Salkind (Ed.), Encyclopedia of Measurement and Statistics (pp. 792-795). Thousand Oaks, CA: Sage

Adler NE, Newman K. (2002) Socio-economic disparities in health: pathways and policies. Health Aff. 2002;21(2):60–76

Albrecht G, Sartore GM, Connor L, Higginbotham N, Freeman S, Kelly B, et al(2007). Solastalgia: the distress caused by environmental change. Australas Psychiatry. 2007;15(Suppl 1):S95–S98.

Ali, I. (2007). Inequality and the imperative for inclusive growth in Asia. *Asian Development Review, 24*(2), 1-16.

Alvaredo, F., Atkinson, A. B.,Piketty, T., &Saez, E. (2013). The top 1 percent in international and historical perspective. *Journal of Economic Perspectives, 27*(3), 3-20.

Amato, P. R. (2005). The impact of family formation change on the cognitive, social, and emotional well-being of the next generation. *Future of Children, 15(2),* 75-96.

American Academy of Child and Adolescent Psychiatry (AACAP). (2010). *A Guide to Building Collaborative Mental Health Care Partnerships in Pediatric Primary Care.*

American Academy of Pediatrics Policy statement (2013): children, adoles- cents, and the media. Pediatrics. 2013;132(5):958–961. doi: 10.1542/ peds.2013-2656.

American Psychiatric Association. (2000). Diagnostic and Statistical Manual of Mental Disorders (DSM-IV-TR). Washington, DC: American Psychiatric Association.

Andermann, A., CLEAR Collaboration (2016). Taking action on the social determinants of health in clinical practice: a framework for health profession- als. *CMAJ : Canadian Medical Association journal = journal de l'Association medicale canadienne, 188*(17-18), E474-E483.

Andrade, L. H. S. G., Alonso, J.,Mneimneh, Z.,Wells, J. E.,Al-Hamzawi, A. O.,Borges, G., ... Kessler, R. C. (2014). "Barriers to Mental Health Treat- ment: Results from the WHO World Mental Health Surveys." Psychological Medicine,44, 1303–17. doi:10.1017/S0033291713001943

Andréasson, S., Allebeck, P., Engström, A., &Rydberg, U. (1987). Cannabis and schizophrenia. A longitudinal study of Swedish conscripts. Lancet, 2, 1483–6.

Aneshensel CS, Sucoff CA.(1996) The neighborhood context of adolescent mental health. Journal of Health and Social Behavior. 1996;37(4):293–310

Anthony, W. A. (1993). Recovery from Mental Illness: The Guiding Vision of the Mental Health Service System in the 1990s.*Psychosocial Rehabilitation Journal, 16,* 11–23. doi:10.1037/h0095655

Araya, R., Lewis, G., Rojas, G., & Fritsch, R. (2003). Education and income: which is more important for mental health? Journal of Epidemiology and Community Health, 57(7), 501–505. doi.org/10.1136/jech.57.7.501

Arnett,J.(2000).Emergingadulthood:Atheoryofdevelopmentfromthelateteens-throughthetwenties.AmericanPsychologist,55(5),469-480.

Armesto, S. G., Medeiros, H., &Wei, L. (2008). Information Availability for Measuring and Comparing Quality of Mental Health Care across OECD Countries.OECD HealthTechnical Papers, no. 20, OECD Publishing.

Aubry, T., Nelson, G., & Tsemberis, S. (2015). Housing First for

People With Severe Mental Illness Who Are Homeless: A Review of the Research and Findings From the At Home–Chez soi Demonstration Project. Canadian Journal of Psychiatry. Revue Canadienne de Psychiatrie, 60(11), 467–474.

Baggio S, Iglesias, K., Deline, S., Studer, J., Henchoz, Y., Mohler-Kuo, M., &Gmel, G.(2015).Not in education, employment, or training status among young Swiss men. Longitudinal associations with mental health and sub- stance use. *J Adolesc Health,56*, 238–43.

Ball, L., D. Furceri, D. Leigh, and P. Loungani, (2014), The distributional effects of fiscal consolidation, *IMF Working Paper, No. 13/151* (International Monetary Fund).

Balogh, K. N., Mayes, L. C., & Potenza, M. N. (2013). Risk-taking and deci- sion-making in youth: relationships to addiction vulnerability. *Journal of behavioral addictions,* 2(1), 10.1556/JBA.2.2013.1.1.

Baranne, M. L., & Falissard, B. (2018). Global burden of mental disorders among children aged 5-14 years. Child and adolescent psychiatry and mental health, 12, 19. doi:10.1186/s13034-018-0225-4

Barr, V. J., Robinson, S., Marin-Link, B., Underhill, L., Dotts, A., Ravensdale, D., & Salivaras, S. (2003). The expanded chronic care model: an integration of concepts and strategies from population health promotion and the chronic care model. Hosp Q, 7(1), 73–82.

Baxter, A. J., Patton, G., Scott, K. M., Degenhardt, L.,& White ford, H. A. (2013). Global Epidemiology of Mental Disorders: What Are We Missing? PLoS ONE,8(6), 5514.

Beesdo, K., Knappe, S., & Pine, D. S. (2009). Anxiety and Anxiety Disorders in Children and Adolescents: Developmental Issues and Implications for DSM-V. The Psychiatric Clinics of North America, 32(3), 483–524. doi. org/10.1016/j.psc.2009.06.002

Begall, K., & Mills, M. (2011). The Impact of Subjective Work Control, Job Strain and Work–Family Conflict on Fertility Intentions: a European Com- parison. *European Journal of Population,* 27(4), 433–456. doi.org/10.1007/ s10680-011-9244-z

Benach, J.,& Muntaner, C. (2007). Precarious employment and health: develop- ing a research agenda.*J Epidemiol Community Health,61*, 276–277.

Benach. J., Muntaner, C., & Santana, V. (2007). Employment Conditions and Health Inequalities. Final Report to the WHO Commission on Social Determinants of Health (CSDH).

Benach, J., Vives, A., Tarafa, G., Delclos, C., & Muntaner, C. (2016). What should we know about precarious employment and health in 2025? Framing the agenda for the next decade of research. *Int J Epidemiol, 45*(1), 232-238. doi:10.1093/ije/dyv342

Benach, J., Vives, A., Amable, M., Vanroelen, C., Tarafa, G., & Muntaner, C. (2014). Precarious Employment: Understanding an Emerging Social Determinant of Health. *Annual Review of Public Health, 35,* 229–53. doi:10.1146/ annurev-publhealth-032013-182500

Benach, J., Muntaner, C., Chung, H., Solar, O., Santana, V., Friel, S., ... Marmot, M. (2010). The Importance of Government Policies in Reducing Employment Related Health Inequalities. BMJ, 340, 2154.

Benjet, C., Hernández-Montoya, D., Borges, G., Méndez, E., Medina-Mora, M. E., &Aguilar-Gaxiola, S. (2012). Youth who neither study nor work: mental health, education and employment. *Salud Publica Mex,54*(4), 410–7.

Bentley, R., Baker, E., Mason, K., Subramanian, S. V., Kavanagh, A. M. (2011). Association Between Housing Affordability and Mental Health: A Longitu- dinal Analysis of a Nationally Representative Household Survey in Australia, *American Journal of Epidemiology, 174*(7), 753–760. doi.org/10.1093/aje/ kwr161

Bengtsson, E., & Waldenström, D. (2017). Capital Shares and Income Inequality: Evidence from the Long Run. *Journal of Economic History.*

Berg, J. (2015). Labour market institutions: the building blocks of just societies, Ch 1. In J. Berg(ed.), Labour Markets, Institutions and

Inequality Building Just Societies in the 21st Century, ILO

Bhalla, A., &Lapeyre, F. (2004).Towards an Analytical and Operational Frame- work. Poverty and Exclusion in a Global World(2ndEd) (pp. 33-58). London, UK: Palgrave Macmillan.

Bijl, R. V., de Graaf, R., Hiripi, E., Kessler, R. C., Kohn, R., Offord, D. R., ... Wittchen, H. V. (2003). The prevalence of treated and untreated mental disorders in five countries. *Health Affairs*, 22(3),.

Blankenship, K. M., Friedman, S. R., Dworkin, S., & Mantell, J. E. (2006). Structural interventions: concepts, challenges and opportunities for research. Journal of urban health : bulletin of the New York Academy of Medicine, 83(1), 59-72.

Bodenheimer, T., Lo, B., &Casalino, L. (1999). Primary care physicians should be coordinators, not gatekeepers. *JAMA, 281,* 2045–9.

Bramlett, M.D., &Blumberg S.J. (2007). Family structure and children's physical and mental health. *Health Aff,* 26, 549–558. doi:10.1377/hlthaff.26.2.549

Braveman, P., Egerter, S., &Williams, D. R. (2011), The social determinants of health: Coming of age. Annu Rev Public Health, 32,381–98.

Braveman, P., & Gottlieb, L. (2014). The Social Determinants of Health: It's Time to Consider the Causes of the Causes. *Public Health Reports, 129*(Suppl 2), 19–31.

Brennan, P. A., Mednick, S. A., &Hodgins, S. (2000). Major Mental Disorders and Criminal Violence in a Danish Birth Cohort. *Arch Gen Psychiatry,* 57(5), 494-500.

Bodenheimer, T., Lo, B., &Casalino, L.(1999). Primary care physicians should be coordinators, not gatekeepers. *Journal of the American Medical Association, 281*(21), 2045-2049.

Bouchery EE, Harwood HJ, Sacks JJ, Simon CJ, Brewer RD. Economic Costs of Excessive Alcohol Consumption in the U.S., 2006(2011). American Journal of Preventive Medicine.

2011;41(5):516–24. 10.1016/j.amepre.2011.06.045.

Boutayeb, A. (2006). The double burden of communicable and non-communica- ble diseases in developing countries.*Trans R Soc Trop Med HygSee comment in PubMed Commons below Mar, 100*(3), 191-9.

Bruckner, T. A., Scheffler, R. M., Shen, G., Yoon, J., Chisholm, D., Morris, J., ... Saxena, S. (2011). The mental health workforce gap in low- and middle-income countries: a needs-based approach. *Bull World Health Organ,89*(3),184–94.

Burgard, S. A., & Lin, K. Y. (2013). Bad Jobs, Bad Health? How Work and Working Conditions Contribute to Health Disparities. *American Behavioral Scientist, 57*(8). doi.org/10.1177/0002764213487347

Burgard, S. A., Brand, J. E., & House, J. S. (2009). Perceived job insecurity and worker health in the United States. *Social Science & Medicine, 69*(5), 777–785.

Buss, P. M., Ferreira, J. R., & Hoirisch, C. (2014). Health and development in BRICS countries. *Saúde e Sociedade, 23*(2), 390-403.

Campbell, M., Thomson, H., Fenton, C., & Gibson, M. (2016). Lone parents, health, wellbeingand welfare to work: a systematic review of qualitative studies. BMC Public Health, 16, 188. doi.org/10.1186/s12889-016-2880-9

Carcillo, S. et al. (2015), NEET Youth in the Aftermath of the Crisis: Challenges and Policies. *OECD Social, Employment and Migration Working Papers*, No. 164, OECD Publishing. doi.org/10.1787/5js6363503f6-en

Carey, G., Crammond, B., & De Leeuw, E. (2015). Towards health equity: a framework for the application of proportionate universalism. *International journal for equity in health, 14*, 81. doi:10.1186/s12939-015-0207-6

Carr, W., &Wolfe, S. (1976).Unmet needs as socio medical indicators. *Int J Health Serv, 6*(3), 417-30.

Carson, N., Cook, B., & Alegría, M. (2010). Social Determinants of Mental Health Treatment among Haitian, African American and White Youth in Community Health

Centers. *Journal of Health Care for the Poor and Underserved*, 21(2 Suppl), 32–48. doi.org/10.1353/hpu.0.0297

Carter, K. N., Blakely, T., Collings, S., ImlachGunasekara, F., Richardson, K.(2009).What is the association between wealth and mental health? *J Epidemiol Community Health,63*(3), 221-6. doi:10.1136/jech.2008.079483

Carter, K. N., Blakely, T., Collings,Leon, D.A., Walt, G., &Gilson, L. (2001). Recent advances: international perspectives on health inequalities and policy. *BMJ, 322*, 5914.

Castellanos-Ryan, N., O'Leary-Barrett, M., & Conrod, P. J. (2013). Substance-use in Childhood and Adolescence: A Brief Overview of Developmental Processes and their Clinical Implications. *Journal of the Canadian Academy of Child and Adolescent Psychiatry = Journal de l'Academie canadienne de psychiatrie de l'enfant et de l'adolescent, 22*(1), 41-6.

CBO. (2011). Trends in the Distribution of Household Income Between 1979 and 2007. Retrieved from https://www.cbo.gov/publication/42729

Chandola, T., Martikainen, P., Bartley, M., Lahelma, E., Marmot, M., Michikazu, S., ... Kagamimori, S. (2004). Does conflict between home and work explain the effect of multiple roles on mental health? A comparative study of Finland, Japan, and the UK. *IntJEpidemiol,33*, 884–893.

Charlson, F. J., Baxter, A. J., Cheng, H. G., Shidhaye, R., & White ford, H. A. (2016). The burden of mental, neurological, and substance use disorders in China and India: a systematic analysis of community representative epidemi- ological studies. *Lancet, 388*(10042), 376-389.

Chesney, E., Goodwin, G. M., & Fazel, S. (2014). Risks of all-cause and suicide mortality in mental disorders: a meta-review. *World psychiatry : official journal of the World Psychiatric Association (WPA), 13*(2), 153-60.

Chisholm, D., and S. Saxena. 2012. "Cost Effectiveness of Strategies to Combat Neuropsychiatric Conditions in Sub-Saharan Africa and South East Asia: Mathematical Modelling Study." BMJ 344:e609. doi:10.1136/bmj.e609.

Chisholm, D., K. A. Raykar, N. Meggido, I. Nigam, A. Nigam, K. B. Strand, A. Colson, A. Fekadu, and S. Verguet. 2015. "Universal Health Coverage for Mental, Neurological, and Substance Use Disorders: An Extended Cost-Ef- fectiveness Analysis." In Disease Control Priorities (third edition): Volume 4, Mental, Neurological, and Substance Use Disorders, edited by V. Patel, D. Chisholm, T. Dua, R. Laxminarayan, and M. E. Medina-Mora. Washington, DC: World Bank

Chuang YC, Chuang KY, Yang TH. Social cohesion matters in health. *Int J Equity Health.* 2013 Oct 28;12:87.

Cingano, F. (2014). Trends in Income Inequality and Its Impact on Economic Growth.*OECD SEM Working Paper* No. 163. Retrieved from www.oecd.org/ els/workingpapers

Clougherty, J. E., Souza, K., &Cullen, M. R. (2010). Work and Its Role in Shaping the Social Gradient in Health. *Annals of the New York Academy of Sciences, 1186*, 102–24.

Coder B, Freyer-Adam J, Lau K, Riedel J, Rumpf HJ, Meyer C, John U, Hapke U(2009): Reported beverage consumed and alcohol-related diseases among male hospital in-patients with problem drinking. Alcohol Alcohol. 2009 Mar-Apr;44(2):216-21. doi: 10.1093/alcalc/agn113. Epub 2009 Jan 12.

Coles, B., Hutton, S., Bradshaw, J., Graig, G., Godfrey, C.,& Johson, J. (2002). Literature Review on the Costs Resulting From Social Exclusion Among Young People Aged 16-18. Report to the DfES, Social Policy Research Unit, University of York, DfES 1805.

Commission on Social Determinants of Health, World Health Organization (WHO)(2008), Closing the Gap in a Generation: Health

Equity Through Action on the Social Determinants of Health (Geneva: WHO, 2008).

Commonwealth Fund. (2012). "Young, Uninsured, and in Debt: Why Young Adults Lack Health Insurance and How the Affordable Care Act Is Help- ing—Findings from the Commonwealth Fund Health Insurance Tracking Survey of Young Adults, 2011." *Issue Brief.* Retrieved fromhttp://www.com- monwealthfund.org/publications/issue-briefs/2012/jun/young-adults-2012

Community Preventive Services Task Force (CPSTF). (2012). Recommendation from the Community Preventive Services Task Force for Use of Collaborative Care for the Management of Depressive Disorders.*American Journal of Preventive Medicine, 42,* 521–24. doi:10.1016/j.amepre.2012.01.010

Connor JP, Haber PS, Hall WD. Alcohol use disorders (2016) Lancet.2016;387(10022):988–998

Connor J, Kydd R, Shield K, Rehm J.(2015): The burden of disease and injury attributable to alcohol in New Zealanders under 80 years of age: marked disparities by ethnicity and sex. N Z Med J. 2015 Feb 20;128(1409):15-28.

Connor JP, Haber PS, Hall WD. Alcohol use disorders. Lancet. 2016; 387(10022):988–998.

Corak, M. (2013). Income inequality, equality of opportunity, and intergenerational mobility. Journal of Economic Perspectives, 27(3), 79-102.

Corrigan, P. W. (2004). How Stigma Interferes with Mental Health Care. *American Psychologist, 59,* 614–25. doi:10.1037/0003-066X.59.7.614

Corrigan, P. W., &Penn, D. L. (1999). Lessons from Social Psychology on Discrediting Psychiatric Stigma. *American Psychologist, 54,* 765–76. doi:10.1037/0003-066X.54.9.765

Corrigan, P.W., Morris, S. B.,Michaels, P. J., Rafacz, J. D., &Rüsch, N. (2012). Challenging the Public Stigma of Mental Illness: A Meta-Analysis of Outcome Studies. *Psychiatric Services, 63,* 963–73.

doi:10.1176/appi. ps.201100529

Costello, E. J., Compton, S. N., Keeler, G. &Angold, A. (2003). Relationships between poverty and psychopathology: A natural experiment. *JAMA, 290*, 2023–2029

Costello EJ(2016). Early detection and prevention of mental health problems: developmental epidemiology and systems of support. J Clin Child Adolesc 2016;45:710–7. 10.1080/15374416.2016.1236728

Couture, S. M., &Penn, D. L. (2003). Interpersonal Contact and the Stigma of Mental Illness: A Review of the Literature. *Journal of Mental Health, 12*, 291–305. doi:10.1080/09638231000118276

Cranford, C.J., Vosko, L.F., & Zukewich, N. (2003). Precarious Employment in the Canadian Labour Market: A Statistical Portrait. *Just Labour, 3*, 6-22.

Crompton M T and Shim R S (2015): The Social Determinants of Mental Health, Focus Vol. 13, No. 4, Fall 2015, 419-425

CSDH. (2008). Closing the gap in a generation: health equity through action on the social determinants of health. Final Report of the Commission on Social Determinants of Health. Geneva, World Health Organization.

Cummings, J. R., Wen, H.,&Druss, B. J. (2013). Improving Access to Mental Health Services for Youth in the United States.*JAMA, 309*, 553–54. doi:10.1001/jama.2013.437

Dabla-Norris, E., Kochhar, K., Suphaphiphat, N.,Ricka, F., &Tsounta, E. (2015). *Causes and Consequences of Income Inequality: A Global Perspective*, IMF Staff Discussion Note.

Danziger, S., &Ratner, D. (2010). Labor market outcomes and the transition to adulthood. *Future Child, 20*(1), 133-58.

Dashiff, C., DiMicco, W., Myers, B., & Sheppard, K. (2009). Poverty and adolescent mental health. *Journal of Child and Adolescent Psychiatric Nursing, 22(1)*, 23-32.

Davidson, L., O'Connell, M., Tondora, J., Styron, T., &Kangas,

K. (2006). The top ten concerns about recovery encountered in mental health system transformation. *Psychiatric Services, 57*, 640–645.

Degenhardt L, Hall W.(2012) Extent of illicit drug use and dependence, and their contribution to the global burden of disease. Lancet. 2012;379(9810):55–70.

Degenhardt, L., Whiteford, H. A., Ferrari, A. J., Baxter, A. J., Charlson, F. J., Hall WD, …Vos, T. (2013). Global burden of disease attributable to illicit drug use and dependence: findings from the Global Burden of Disease Study 2010. *Lancet, 382,* 1564–74.

Degenhardt L, Stockings E, Patton G, Hall WD, Lynskey M. (2016) The increas- ing global health priority of substance use in young people. The Lancet Psychiatry. 2016;3: 251–264. 10.1016/S2215-0366(15)00508-8

de Graaf, R., Bijl, R. V., Smit, F., Vollebergh, W. A., &Spijker, J. (2002). Risk factors for 12-month comorbidity of mood, anxiety, and substance use dis- orders: findings from the Netherlands Mental Health Survey and Incidence Study.*Am J Psychiatry, 159*(4), 620-9.

De Hert, M., Cohen, D.,Bobes, J., Cetkovich-Bakmas, M., Leucht, S., Ndetei,

D. M.,… Correll, C. U. (2011a). Physical Illness in Patients with Severe Mental Disorders. I. Prevalence, Impact of Medications and Disparities in Health Care.*World Psychiatry, 10,* 52–77. doi:10.1002/j.2051-5545.2011. tb00014.x

De Hert, M., Cohen, D., Bobes, J., Cetkovich-Bakmas, M., Leucht, S., Ndetei, D. M.,… Correll, C. U. (2011b). Physical Illness in Patients with Severe Mental Disorders. II. Barriers to Care, Monitoring and Treatment Guide- lines, Plus Recommendations at the System and Individual Level." *World Psychiatry, 10,* 138–51. doi:10.1002/j.2051-5545.2011.tb00036.x

De Hert, M., Correll, C. U., Bobes, J., Cetkovich-Bakmas, M., Cohen, D., Asai, I., … Leucht, S. (2011). Physical illness in patients with severe mental disorders. I. Prevalence, impact of medications and disparities in health care. *World Psychiatry, 10*(1), 52–77.

De Witte, H. (1999). Job Insecurity and Psychological Well-being: Review of the Literature and Exploration of Some Unresolved Issues. *European Journal Of Work And Organizational Psychology, 8*(2), 155–177.

de Lange, A., Taris, T. W., Kompier, M. A. J., Houtman, I. L. D., &Bongers, P. M. (2005). Different mechanisms to explain the reversedeffects of mental health on work characteristics. *Scand J Work Environ Health, 31*(1), 3-14.

De Maio, F. G. (2007). Income inequality measures. *Journal of Epidemiology and Community Health, 61*(10), 849–852. doi.org/10.1136/jech.2006.052969

Demyttenaere, K., Bruffaerts, R., Posada-Villa, J., Gasquet, I., Kovess, V., Lepine, J. P.,… Chatterji, S. (2004).WHO World Mental Health Survey Consor- tium. Prevalence, severity, and unmet need for treatment of mental disorders in the World Health Organization World Mental Health Surveys. *JAMA, 291,* 2581–2590.

Desjarlais, R., Eisenberg, L., Good, B., &Kleinman, A. (1995). *World Mental Health: Problems and Priorities in Low-Income Countries.* Oxford: Oxford University Press.

Development Services GroupInc. (2016).Behind the Term: Serious Mental Illness.

Dieterich, M., Irving, C. B., Park B., & Marshall, M. (2010). "Intensive Case Management for Severe Mental Illness." *The Cochrane Database of Systematic Reviews,10*, CD007906.

Dieterich, M., Irving, C. B., Bergman, H., Khokhar, M. A., Park, B., Mar- shall, M. (2017). Intensive case management for severe mental illness. Cochrane Database of *Systematic Reviews, 1, Art. No.: CD007906. doi:10.1002/14651858.CD007906.pub3*

Dohrenwend, B. P., Levav, I., Shrout, P. E., Schwartz, S., Naveh, G., Link, B. G., … Stueve, A.(1992). Socioeconomic status and psychiatric disorders: The causation-selection issue. *Science, 255,* 946–952.

Dooley, D., Prause, J., & Ham-Rowbottom, K. A. (2000). Under-employment and Depression: Longitudinal Relationships. *Journal of Health & Social Behaviour, 41*, 421–36. doi:10.2307/2676295

Drake, R. E., Mueser, K. T., & Brunette, M. F. (2007). Management of persons with co-occurring severe mental illness and substance use disorder: program implications. *World psychiatry : official journal of the World Psychiatric Association (WPA), 6*(3), 131–136.

Durlak JA, Wells AM(1997). Primary prevention mental health programs for children and adolescents: a meta-analytic review. Am J Community Psychol. 1997;25:115–152. doi: 10.1023/A:1024654026646.

Durlak JA, Wells AM(1998). Evaluation of indicated preventive intervention (secondary prevention) mental health programs for children and adolescents. Am J Community Psychol. 1998;26: 775–802.

Eaton, J., McCay, L., Semrau, M., Chatterjee, S., Baingana, F., Araya, R., ... Saxena, S. (2011).Scale up of services for mental health in low-income and middle-income countries. *Lancet, 378*(9802), 1592–603.

Egede LE(2oo4): Diabetes, major depression, and functional disability among U.S. adults. Diabetes Care 2004;27:421–8.

Eibner, C., Sturn, R., &Gresenz, C. R. (2004). Does relative deprivation predict the need for mental health services?. *The Journal of Mental Health Policy and Economics, 7*, 167-175.

Eibner, C., &Evans, W. N. (2005). Relative deprivation, poor health habits, and mortality. *J Hum Resour, 40*, 591-620.

Elizabeth Hartney(2018): A Guide to DSM 5 Criteria for Substance Use Disorders Symptoms Used to Diagnose Substance Use Disorders, Verywell Mind, https://www.verywellmind.com/ dsm-5-criteria-for-substance-use-disorders-21926

Elliott, M.&Krivo, L.(1991). Structural determinants of homelessness in the United States. *Social Problems, 38*(1),113–31.

Ennis, S. F., Gonzaga, P.,& Pike, C. (2017). Inequality: A Hidden Cost of Market Power. Retrieved from www.oecd.org/daf/competition/inequality-a-hidden- cost-of-market-power.htm

Erskine, H. E., Moffitt, T. E., Copeland, W. E., Costello, E. J., Ferrari, A. J., Pat- ton, G., Degenhardt, L., Vos, T., White ford, H. A., … Scott, J. G. (2014). A heavy burden on young minds: the global burden of mental and substance use disorders in children and youth. *Psychological medicine, 45*(7), 1551-63.

European Observatory on Homelessness. (2014): Extent and Profile of Homeless- ness in European Member States EOH Comparative Studies on Homeless- ness, A Statistical Update, Brussels – December 2014.

European Parliamentary Research Service. (2016).Poverty in the European Union, The Crisis and the aftermath. EuroStat Statistics Explained. (2016). People at risk of poverty or social exclusion,

Evans, J., &Gibb, E. (2009). *Moving from Precarious Employment to Decent Work.* International Labour Office; Global Union Research Network (GURN) Discussion Paper no. 13. Geneva: ILO.

Fagan, C., Lyonette, C., Smith, M.,&Saldaña-Tejeda, A.(2012). The influence of working time arrangements on work-life integration or 'balance': a review of the international evidence, International Labour Office, Conditions of Work and Employment Branch. - Geneva: ILO.

Falk, R.F., &Miller, N.B.(1992). *A Primer for Soft Modeling.*Akron, Ohio:The University of Akron Press.

Farahani, H.A., Rahiminezhad, A., Same, L., 2010. A Comparison of Partial Least Squares (PLS) and Ordinary Least Squares (OLS) regressions in pre- dicting of couples mental health based on their communicational patterns. Procedia-Social Behav. Sci. 5, 1459–1463.

Farkas, M. (2007). The Vision of Recovery Today: What It Is and What It Means for Services. *World Psychiatry, 6*, 68-74.

Fazel, S., Gulati, G., Linsell, L., Geddes, J. R., &Grann, M. (2009). Schizo- phrenia and violence:systematic review and meta-analysis. *PLoS Med, 6*(8), e1000120-10.1371/journal.pmed.1000120.

Ferrie, J. E. (2001). Is job insecurity harmful to health? *Journal of the Royal Society of Medicine, 94*(2), 71–76.

Ferrie,J. E. (ed). (2004).WORK STRESS AND HEALTH: the Whitehall II study. Retrieved from https://www.ucl.ac.uk/whitehallII/pdf/wii-booklet

Ferrie, J. E., Marmot, M. G., Griffiths, J., Ziglio, E. (eds.).(1999). Labour market changes and job insecurity: A challenge for social welfare and health promo- tion Copenhagen: WHO Regional Publications, European Series, No 81.

Ferrie, J. E., Shipley, M. J., Stansfeld, S. A., & Marmot, M. G. (2002). Effects of chronic job insecurity and change in job security on self-reported health, minor psychiatric morbidity, physiological measures, and health related behaviours in British civil servants: the Whitehall II study. *Journal of Epidemiology and Community Health, 56*(6), 450–454.

Ferrie, J. E., Westerlund, H., Virtanen, M., Vahtera, J.,& Kivimki, M. (2008). Flexible labor markets and employee health.*Scandinavian Journal of Work, Environment and Health, Supplement,6*, 98–110.

Fisher, M., &Baum, F.(2010). The social determinants of mental health: implica- tions for research and health promotion. *Aust N Z J Psychiatry,44*,1057-63.

Foot, C., Naylor, C., &Imison, C. (2010). *The quality of GP diagnosis and referral.* London: King›s Fund.

Forrest, C. B., Glade, G. B., Baker, A. E., Bocian, A., von Schrader, S., &Star- field, B. (2000). Coordination of specialty referrals and physician satisfaction with referral care. Arch Pediatr Adolesc Med, 154, 499–506.

Forrest, C. B., Nutting, P. A., von Schrader, S., Rohde, C., &Starfield, B. (2006). Primary care physician specialty referral decision making: Patient, physician, and health care system determinants. *Med Decis Making, 26*, 76–85.

Fisher, M.,& Baum, F. (2010). The social determinants of mental health: implications for research and health promotion.*Aust N Z J*

Psychia- try, See comment in PubMed Commons below 44(12), 1057-63. doi: 10.3109/00048674.2010.509311

Fleury, M.J., Grenier, G., &Vallée, C. (2014). Evaluation of the implementation of the Montreal at home/chez soi project. *BMC Health Services Research, 14,* 557.

Förster, M. (2015).Inequality in The OECD Area: Trends, Causes, Conse- quences and Remedies OECD Social Policy Division. Retrieved fromwww.oecd.org/social/ inequality-and-poverty.htm

Frazer, H., & Marlier, E. (2010).*In-work poverty and labour market segmentation in the EU.* CEPS/INSTEAD, 2010, coll. European Network of Independent Experts on Social Inclusion n2010-02.

Freyd, J., &Birrell, P. (2013). *Blind to Betrayal: Why we fool ourselves we aren't being fooled.* John Wiley & Sons.

Friedli, L. (2009). *Mental Health, Resilience, and Inequalities—A Report for WHO Europe and the Mental Health Foundation London/ Copenhagen: Mental Health Foundation and WHO Europe.*

Friese B, Grube JW(2010). Youth Drinking Rates and Problems: A Comparison of European Countries and the United States. U.S. Department of Justice, Office of Juvenile Justice and Delinquency Prevention 2010

Frone, M. R. (2000).Work-Family Conflict and Employee Psychiatric Disorders:: The National Comorbidity Survey.*Journal of Applied Psychology, 85,* 888-895.

Funk, M., Drew, N., & Knapp, M. (2012).Mental health, poverty and development. *Journal of Public Mental Health, 11*(4), 166-185.

Fukuda-Parr, S. (2003).The Human Development Paradigm: Operationalizing Sen'sIdeas on Capabilities. *Feminist Economics, 9*(2-3), 301-317.

Funk, M., Drew, N., & Knapp, M. (2012). Mental Health, Poverty, and Development. *Journal of Public Mental Health, 11,* 166–85.

Gagnon, M.-A. (2014). *A Roadmap to a Rational Pharmacare Policy in Canada*. Canadian Federation of Nurses Unions (accessed March 22, 2016). Retrieved from https://nursesunions.ca/sites/default/files/pharmacare_report.pdf

Gadermann, A. M., Alonso, J., Vilagut, G., Zaslavsky, A. M., & Kessler, R.

C. (2012). Comorbidity and disease burden in the National Comorbidity Survey Replication (NCS-R). *Depression and anxiety, 29*(9), 797-806.

Gallie, D., Felstead, A., Green, F.,&Inanc, H. (2016). The hidden face of job insecurity. *Work, Employment & Society*. doi:10.1177/0950017015624399

Garcia, A., S., Medeiros, H., &Wei, L. (2008). Information Availability for Measuring and Comparing Quality of Mental Health Care across OECD Countries.*OECD Health Technical Papers* No. 20. OECD Publishing. doi. org/10.1787/237827772222

Garrett, D. G. (2012). The Business Case for Ending Homelessness: Having a Home Improves Health, Reduces Healthcare Utilization and Costs. *American Health & Drug Benefits, 5*(1), 17–19.

Garthwaite, P. H. (1994). An interpretation of partial least squares. *Journal of the American Statistical Association, 89*(425) pp. 122–127.

GBD 2015 Eastern Mediterranean Region Collaborators. (2017). The burden of mental disorders in the Eastern Mediterranean region, 1990–2015: findings from the global burden of disease 2015 study. *International Journal of Public Health,7.*

GBD 2015 Disease and Injury Incidence and Prevalence Collaborators (Lan- cet 2016);

GBD 2016 Disease and Injury Incidence and Prevalence Collaborators (Lan- cet 2017)

GBD 2016 Alcohol Collaborators (2018). Alcohol use and burden for 195 coun- tries and territories, 1990-2016: a systematic analysis for the Global Burden of Disease Study 2016. *Lancet (London, England), 392*(10152), 1015-1035.

GBD 2016 Alcohol and Drug Use Collaborators (20018). The global burden of disease attributable to alcohol and drug use in 195 countries and territories, 1990–2016: a systematic analysis for the Global Burden of Disease Study 2016. The Lancet Psychiatry Epub (2018)

GBD 2017 Disease and Injury Incidence and Prevalence Collaborators (2018). Global, regional, and national incidence, prevalence, and years lived with disability for 354 diseases and injuries for 195 countries and territories, 1990-2017: a systematic analysis for the Global Burden of Disease Study 2017. *Lancet (London, England), 392*(10159), 1789-1858.

Gervais, M. (2013). The Rationale for Integrating Mental Health Care within Comprehensive Primary Care Setting. Mental Health Commission of Canada Article 3. Retrieved from http://www.mentalhealthcommission.ca/ English/document-type/article?page=1

Godfrey, C., Hutton, S., Bradshaw, J., Coles, B., Craig, G., & Johnson, J. (2002). Estimating the cost of being 'not in education, employment or training' at age 16-18. Research ReportDepartment for Education and Skills, 346.

Goetzel RZ, Hawkins K, Ozminkowski RJ, Wang S(2003):The health and productivity cost burden of the "top 10" physical and mental health conditions affecting six large U.S. employers in 1999. J Occup Environ Med 2003; 45 (01) 5-14

Gold, R., Kennedy, B., Connell, F., &Kawachi, I. (2002). Teen births, inco- meinequality, and social capital: developing an understanding of thecausal pathway. *Health Place, 8,* 77–83.

Goldberg, D. & Huxley, P. (1980).*Mental Illness in the Community.* Tavistock.

Goodrich, D. E., Kilbourne, A. M., Nord, K. M., & Bauer, M. S. (2013). Mental Health Collaborative Care and Its Role in Primary Care Settings. *Current Psychiatry Reports, 15*(8), 383. doi.org/10.1007/s11920-013-0383-2

Gordon, R. (2015). Secular stagnation: A supply-side view. *Amer-*

ican Economic Review: Papers and Proceedings, 105(5), 54-59.

Gordon R. S. (1983). An operational classification of disease prevention. Public health reports (Washington, D.C. : 1974), 98(2), 107-9.

Gore. F. M., Bloem, P. J. N., Patton, G. C., Ferguson, J., Joseph, V., Coffey, C., ... Mathers,Gottschalk, P., &Smeeding, T. M. (1997). Cross-National Comparisons of Earnings and Income Inequality. *Journal of Economic Literature, 35*(2),633-687.

Gore F.M., Bloem P.J.N., Patton G.C., Ferguson J., Joseph V., Coffey C.(2011): Global burden of disease in young people aged 10–24 years: a systematic analysis. The Lancet. 2011;377:2093–2102.

Grant B. F., Stinson F. S., Dawson D. A., Chou S. P., Dufour M. C., Compton W., et al. (2004). Prevalence and co-occurrence of substance use disorders and independent mood and anxiety disorders - Results from the national epidemiologic survey on alcohol and related conditions. *Arch. Gen. Psychiatry* 61 807–816. 10.1001/archpsyc.61.8.807

Grigg, David(2004): Wine, Spirits and Beer: World Patterns of Consumption, Geography;Apr2004, Vol. 89 Issue 2, p99-110

Gruskin, S., Plafker, K., &Smith-Estelle, A. (2001). Understanding and Responding to Youth Substance Use: The Contribution of a Health and Human Rights Framework. *American Journal of Public Health, 91*(12), 1954-1963.

Grumbach, K., Selby, J.V., Damberg, C., Bindman, A.B., Quesenberry, C., Truman, A., & Uratsu, C. (1999). Resolving the gatekeeper conundrum: What patients value in primary care and referrals to specialists. *JAMA,282*(3),261–266.

Gucciardi, E., Celasun, N., &Stewart, D. E. (2004). Single-mother families in Canada. *Can J Public Health,95*, 70–3.4

Guo, J., Hawkins, J. D., Hill, K. G., & Abbott, R. D. (2001). Childhood and adolescent predictors of alcohol abuse and dependence in young adulthood. *Journal of studies on alcohol, 62*(6), 754-62.

Hahn R, Fuqua-Whitley D, Wethington H, et al. and the Task Force on Commu- nity Preventive Services. Effectiveness of universal school-based programs to prevent violent and aggressive behavior: a systematic review. Am J Prev Med 2007;33(Suppl):S114--S129.

Handren, L. (2015). Unfilled Prescriptions: The Drug Coverage Gap in Canada's Health Care System, Renewing Canada's Social Architecture (accessed March 22, 2016). Retrieved from http://social-architecture.ca/wp-content/uploads/ UnfilledPrescriptions.pdf

Hawkins, J. D., Catalano, R., Miller, J. (1992). Risk and protective factors for alcohol and other drug problems in adolescence and early adulthood: implications for substance use prevention. *Psychol Bull,12*, 64–105.

Hermann, R. C., Mattke, S. and the members of the OECD Mental Health Care Panel. (2004). "Selecting Indicators for the Quality of Mental Health Care at the Health Systems Level in OECD Countries." *OECD Health Technical Papers* No. 17. OECD Publishing.

Herrman H, Saxena S , & Moodie R (Eds.)(2005), Promoting mental health: Concepts, emerging evidence and practice Geneva: World Health Organization

Hobson. B. (2013).*Worklife Balance: The Agency and Capabilities Gap, Ch 1*, Published to Oxford Scholarship Online: January 2014, doi:10.1093/acprof: oso/9780199681136.001.0001

Hudson, C. G. (2005). Socioeconomic Status and Mental Illness: Tests of the Social Causation and Selection Hypotheses. American Journal of Orthopsychiatry, 75, 3–18. doi:10.1037/0002-9432.75.1.3

Hyman, J., Scholarios, D., & Baldry, C. (2005). Getting on or getting by? Employee flexibility and coping strategies for home and work. Work Employment and Society, 19(4), 705-725.

ILO. (2011).Policies and regulations to combat precarious employment. Retrieved from http://www.ilo.org/wcmsp5/groups/public/---ed_dialogue/ actrav/documents/meetingdocument/wcms_164286.pdf ILO. (2012a). The strategy of the International Labour Organization. Social security for all: Building social protection floors and comprehensive social security systems (Geneva).

ILO. (2012b). Social protection assessment based national dialogue: Towards a nationally definedsocial protection floor in Indonesia (Jakarta).

ILO. (2013): Decent work indicators : guidelines for producers and users of statistical and legal framework indicators: ILO manual: second version / International Labour Office. –Geneva: ILO. Retrieved fromhttp://www.ilo. org/wcmsp5/groups/public/---dgreports/---integration/documents/publica- tion/wcms_229374.pdf

International Labour Organization (ILO). (2014). Global Employment Trends 2014: Risk of a Jobless Recovery? Geneva: International Labour Office.

International Labour Organization (ILO). (2015a). *Global Wage Report 2014/15: Wages and Income Inequality.* Geneva: International Labour Office.

ILO.(2015b).World Employment and Social Outlook: The Changing Nature of Jobs", 2015.

ILO. (2015c). Non-standard form of employment, Report for discussion at the Meeting of Experts on Non-Standard Forms of Employment (Geneva, 16–19 February 2015).

ILO. (2016).Non-standard employment around the world: Understanding challenges, shaping prospects International Labour Office – Geneva: ILO. Institute for Health Metrics and Evaluation (IHME) (2018). Findings from the Global Burden of Disease Study 2017. Seattle, WA: IHME, 2018.

Institute of Medicine (IOM). (2006). *Improving the Quality of Health Care for Mental and Substance Use Conditions.* Washington, DC: National Academy Press.

Institute of Work and Health. (2009). "Unemployment and Mental Health." Issue Briefing (accessed March 22, 2016). Retrieved from http://www.iwh. on.ca/briefings/unemployment-and-mental-health.

Institute of Medicine (US) Committee on Prevention of Mental

Disorders(1994); Mrazek PJ, Haggerty RJ, editors. Reducing Risks for Mental Disorders: Frontiers for Preventive Intervention Research. Washington (DC): National Academies Press (US); 1994. 7, Illustrative Preventive Intervention Research Programs. Available from: https://www.ncbi.nlm.nih.gov/books/ NBK236314/

Jacka, F. N., Reavley, N. J., Jorm, A. F., Toumbourou, J. W., Lewis, A. J., & Berk, M.(2013). Prevention of common mental disorders: what can we learn from those who have gone before and where do we go next? Aust N Z J Psychia- try,47, 920-9.

Jacobson, M., & Occhino, F.(2012b). "Labor's Declining Share of Income and Rising Inequality." Federal Reserve Bank of Cleveland.

Jaffee, S. R., & Price, T. S. (2007). Gene-environment correlations: a review of the evidence and implications for prevention of mental illness. Molecular psychiatry, 12(5), 432-42.

Jaumotte, F., & Buitron, C. O. (2015). "Inequality and Labor Market Institutions", IMF working paper.

Jenkins, R., Lancashire, S., McDaid, D., Samyshkin, Y., Green, S., Watkins, J., ... Aturn, R.(2007). Mental health reform in the Russian Federation: an integrated approach to achieve social inclusion and recovery. *B World Health Organ,85*, 858–66.

Jorm, A. F. (2000). Mental Health Literacy: Public Knowledge and Beliefs about Mental Disorders. *The British Journal of Psychiatry, 177*, 396–401. doi:10.1192/bjp.177.5.396

Jorm, A. F., Patten, S. B., Brugha, T. S., & Mojtabai, R. (2017). Has increased provision of treatment reduced the prevalence of common mental disorders? Review of the evidence from four countries. *World Psychiatry, 16*(1), 90–99. doi.org/10.1002/wps.20388

Johnson, S. L., Leedom, L. J., &Muhtadie, L. (2012). The Dominance Behavioral System and Psychopathology: Evidence from Self-Report, Observational, and Biological Studies. *Psychological Bulletin, 138*(4), 692–743. doi.org/10.1037/ a0027503

Kaiser Commission. (2011). "The Uninsured and the Difference Health Insurance Makes". Retrieved from www.kff.org/uninsured/

upload/1420-13.pdf

Kakuma, R. , Minas, H., Van Ginneken, N., Dal Poz, M. R., Desiraju, K., Morris, J. E., ...Scheffler, R. M. (2011).Human resources for mental health care: current situation and strategies for action. *The Lancet, 378*(9803), 1654-1663.

Kalleberg, A. (2006). "Non-standard employment relations and Labour Market inequality: Cross-national patterns" in G. Therborn, G. (ed.): Inequalities of the World (pp.136–161). London: Verso.

Kalleberg,A. L. (2009a). Precarious Work, Insecure Workers: Employment Relations in Transition. *American Sociological Review,74*, 1.

Kalleberg, A. L. (2009b). 2008 Presidential Address: Precarious Work, Insecure Workers: Employment Relations in Transition. *American Sociological Review,74*,1-22.

Kalleberg, A. (2011). *Good jobs, bad jobs: The rise of polarized and precarious employment systems in the United States, 1970s to 2000s.*New York: Russell Sage Foundation.

Kalleberg, A. L. (2014).Measuring Precarious Work, A Working Paper Of The EINet Measurement Group, University of North Carolina at Chapel Hill November, 2014.

Kalleberg, A. L., Reskin, B. F., &Hudson, K.(2000). Bad Jobs in America: Standard and Nonstandard Employment Relations and Job Quality in the United States. *American Sociological Review,65*(2), 256– 278.

Kalra G, Christodoulou G, Jenkins R, Tsipas V, Christodoulou N, LecicTosevski D, et al(2012). Mental health promotion: Guidance and strategies. Eur Psychiatry 2012;27:81-86

Karanikolos, M., Mladovsky, P., Cylus, J., Thomson, S., Basu, S., Stuckler, D., ... McKee, M. (2013). Financial crisis, austerity, and health in Europe. *Lancet,381*, 1323–31.

Kataoka, S. H., Zhang, L., &Wells, K. B. (2002).Unmet need for mental health care among U.S. children: variation by ethnicity and insurance status.*Am J Psychiatry, 159*(9), 1548-55.

Katon, W. J., &Unützer, J. (2013). Health Reform and the Affordable Care Act: The Importance of Mental Health Treatment to Achieving the Triple Aim.*Journal of Psychosomatic Research, 74*, 533–37. doi:10.1016/j. jpsychores.2013.04.005

Katon, W. J., Lin, E. H. B., Von Korff, M., Ciechanowski, P., Ludman, E. J.,Young, B.,…McCulloch, D. (2010). Collaborative Care for Patients with Depression and Chronic Illnesses. *New England Journal of Medicine, 363*, 2611–20. doi:10.1056/NEJMoa1003955

Kaur, S., Sullivan, T.,Laupacis, A., &Petch, J. (2014). Canadian Provinces Take First Steps towards Lower Drug Prices." Healthy Debate (accessed March 22, 2016). Retrieved from http://healthydebate.ca/2014/10/topic/cost-of-care/ pan-canadian-pharmaceutical-alliance

Keeley B 2007, Human Capital How What You Know Shapes Your Life, OECD Insight

Kessler, R. C., Berglund, P., Demler, O., Jin, R., Merikangas, K. R., Walters, E. E. (2005a). Lifetime prevalence and age-of-onset distributions of dsm-iv disorders in the national comorbidity survey replication. *Arch. Gen. Psychia- try, 62*, 593–602. doi:10.1001/archpsyc.62.6.593

Kessler, R. C., Angermeyer, M., Anthony, J. C., De Graaf, R., Demyttenaere, K., Gasquet, I., … Ustun, T. B. (2007). Lifetime prevalence and age-of-onset distributions of mental disorders in the World Health Organization's World Mental Health Survey Initiative. *World Psychiatry, 6*(3), 168–176.

Kessler, R. C., Merikangas, K. R., Berglund, P., Eaton, W. W.,Koretz, D. S., &Walters, E. E. (2003). Mild disorders should not be eliminated from the DSM-V. *Arch Gen Psychiatry, 60*, 1117-1122.

Kessler, R. C., Demler, O., Frank, R. G., Olfson, M., Pincus, H. A., Walters,

Kessler, R. C., Chiu, W. T., Demler, O., &Walters, E. E.(2005c). Prevalence, Severity, and Comorbidity of 12-Month DSM-IV Disorders in the National Comorbidity Survey Replication. *Arch Gen Psych-*

iatry, 62(6), 617-627. doi:10.1001/archpsyc.62.6.617

Kessler, R. C., Amminger, G. P., Aguilar-Gaxiola, S., Alonso, J., Lee, S., &Ustun, T. B. (2007). Age of onset of mental disorders: A review of recent literature. *Current Opinion in Psychiatry,* 20(4), 359–364. doi.org/10.1097/ YCO.0b013e32816ebc8c

Kessler, Ü. (Eds.).(2008). *The WHO World Mental Health Surveys:- Global Perspec- tives on the Epidemiology of Mental Disorders.* Cambridge University Press, New York.

Kessler, R. C., Aguilar-Gaxiola, S.,Alonso, J.,Chatterji, S.,Lee, S., Ormel, J.,Ustün, T. B., & Wang, P.S. (2009). "The Global Burden of Mental Disorders: An Update from the WHO World Mental Health (WMH) Surveys." *Epidemiologia e Psichiatria Sociale,* 18, 23–33. doi:10.1017/ S1121189X00001421

Keyes CL. Promoting and protecting mental health as flourishing(2007): a complementary strategy for improving national mental health. Am Psychol 2007;62:95–108. 10.1037/0003-066X.62.2.95

Khan, L.,&Vaheesan, S. (2017).Market Power and Inequality: The Antitrust Counterrevolution and Its Discontents. *Harvard Law & Policy Review, 11,.*

Kickbusch, I. (2014). BRICS' contributions to the global health agenda. *Bul- letin of the World Health Organization, 92*(6), 463–464. doi.org/10.2471/ BLT.13.127944

Kieling, C., Baker-Henningham, H., Belfer, M., Conti, G., Ertem, I., Omigbo- dun, O., ... Rahman, A.(2011). Child and adolescent-mental health world- wide: evidence for action. *Lancet, 378*(9801), 1515-25.

Kilbourne, A.M., Keyser, D., &Pincus, H. A. (2010). Challenges and Opportu- nities in Measuring the Quality of Mental Health Care. *Canadian Journal of Psychiatry,* 55, 549–57.

Kim,M. (1999).Problems Facing the Working Poor, Future work, Trends and Challenges for Work in the 21st Century, Paper presented at an Economic Policy Institute Symposium on June 15, 1999.

Kirby, J. (2004): Single-parent Families in Poverty.The University of Akron

Kliff, S. (2012). "Seven Facts about America's Mental Health-Care System." Washington Post. December 17, 2012 (accessed March 22, 2016). Retrieved from http://www.washingtonpost.com/news/wonkblog/wp/2012/12/17/ seven-facts-about-americas-mental-healthcare-system/

Knapp, M., Funk, M., Curran, C., Prince, M., Grigg, M., &McDaid, D. (2006). Economic barriers to better mental health practice and policy, *Health Policy and Planning, 21*(3), 157–170.

Knapp, M., Kanavos, P., King, D., &Yesudian, H. M. (2005). Economic Issues in Access to Medications: Schizophrenia Treatment in England.*International Journal of Law & Psychiatry, 28*, 514–31. doi:10.1016/j.ijlp.2005.08.007

Knapp, M., Funk, M., Curran, C., Prince, M., Grigg, M., &McDaid,D. (2006). Economic barriers to better mental health practice and policy. *Health Policy Plan,21*,157–170. doi: 10.1093/heapol/czl003

Knapp, M., McDaid, D., & Mossialos, E. (2007). *Mental health policy and practice across Europe: an overview.* In: Knapp, Martin and McDaid, David and Mossialos, Elias and Thornicroft, Graham, (eds.) Mental Health Policy and Practice Across Europe. European Observatory on Health Systems and Policies series(pp. 1-14). Buckingham, UK:Open University Press.

Kohn, R. (2013). Treatment Gap in the Americas: Technical Document. A Report for the Pan American Health Organization.Retrieved from http://www.paho.org/hq/index.php?option=com_docman&task=doc_download&gid=23178& Itemid=721&lang=en.

Kohn, R., Saxena, S., Levav, I., &Saraceno, B. (2004). The Treatment Gap in Mental Health Care.*Bulletin of the WHO, 82*, 858–66. doi:/ S0042-96862004001100011

Kohn R, Dohrenwend BP, Mirotznik J (1998). Epidemiological findings on selected psychiatric disorders in the general population.

In: Dohrenwend BP, ed. Adversity, stress, and psychopathology. Oxford, Oxford University Press: 235–284.

Krug, E. G., Mercy, J. A., Dahlberg, L. L., &Zwi, A. B. (2002). World report on violence and health. Geneva, World Health Organization. *Lancet, 360*(9339), 1083-8.

Kutcher, S., & McDougall, A. (2009). Problems with access to adolescent mental health care can lead to dealings with the criminal justice system. *Paediatrics & Child Health, 14*(1), 15–18.

Kuruvilla, A., &Jacob, K.S.(2007). Poverty, Social Stress, and Mental Health. *Indian Journal of Medical Research, 126*, 273–78.

Kawachi I, Kennedy BP. Health and social cohesion: why care about income inequality? *BMJ*. 1997 Apr 5;314(7086):1037-40.

Lancet Global Mental Health Group. (2007). Scale Up Services for Mental Disorders: A Call for Action. *Lancet, 370*, 1241–52. The Lancet Commission on global mental health and sustainable development (2018), volume 392, issue 10157, p1553-1598, October 27, 2018 The Lancet

Lajoie J (2015): Understanding the Measurement of Global Burden of Disease, Prepared for the National Collaborating Centre for Infectious Diseases August 2013 Revised February 2015

Lander, L., Howsare, J., & Byrne, M. (2013). The impact of substance use disorders on families and children: from theory to practice. *Social work in public health, 28*(3-4), 194-205.

László, K. D., Pikhart, H., Kopp, M. S., Bobak, M., Pajak, A., Malyutina, S.,… Marmot, M. (2010). Job insecurity and health: A study of 16 European countries. *Social Science & Medicine, 70*(6-3), 867–874. doi.org/10.1016/j. socscimed.2009.11.022

Law Commission of Ontario. (2012). "Vulnerable Workers and Precarious Work." Toronto: Law Commission of Ontario.

Law, M. R., Kratzer, J., & Dhalla, I. A. (2014). The Increasing Efficiency of Private Health Insurance in Canada. *Canadian Medical Association Journal, 186*, E470–E474.

Law, M. R., Cheng, L.,Dhalla, I. A., Heard, D., & Morgan, S. G. (2012). The Effect of Cost on Adherence to Prescription Medications in Canada." *Canadian Medical Association Journal, 184*,297–302. doi:10.1503/cmaj.111270

Lawrence, D., &Kisely, S. (2010). Review: Inequalities in Healthcare Provision for People with Severe Mental Illness. *Journal of Psychopharmacology, 24*, 61–8. doi:10.1177/1359786810382058

Layard, R.Chisolm, D., Patel, V., &Saxena, S. (2013). Mental illness and unhappiness. World Happiness Report 2013. J. F. Helliwell, R. Layard and J. Sachs, D.:39-54.

Leibler, J. H., Nguyen, D. D., León, C., Gaeta, J. M., & Perez, D. (2017).Personal Hygiene Practices among Urban Homeless Persons in Boston, MA. *International Journal of Environmental Research and Public Health, 14*(8), 928.

Lemstra M, Bennett NR, Neudorf C, Kunst A, Nannapaneni U, Warren LM, Kershaw T, Scott CR(2008). A meta-analysis of marijuana and alcohol use by socio-economic status in adolescents aged 10-15 years. Can J Public Health. 2008:172–7

Lê-Scherban, F., Brenner, A. B., &Schoeni, R. F. (2016). Childhood family wealth and mental health in a national cohort of young adults. *SSM Population Health, 2*, 798–806.

Leong, F. T. L., & Lau, A. S. L. (2001). Barriers to providing effective mental health services to Asian Americans. *Mental Health Services Research, 3*(4), 201-214. doi:10.1023/A:1013177014788

Levesque, J.-F., Harris, M. F., & Russell, G. (2013). Patient-centred access to health care: conceptualising access at the interface of health systems and populations. *International Journal for Equity in Health, 12*, 18. doi. org/10.1186/1475-9276-12-18

Levin, C., &Chisholm, D. Cost-Effectiveness and Affordability of Interventions, Policies, and Platforms for the Prevention and Treatment of Mental, Neuro- logical, and Substance Use Disorders. In: Patel V, Chisholm D, Dua T, et al., (eds.). Mental, Neurological, and Substance Use Disorders: Disease Control Priorities, Third Edition

(Volume 4). Washington (DC): The International Bank for Reconstruction and Development / The World Bank; 2016 Mar 14. Chapter 12. Available from: https://www.ncbi.nlm.nih.gov/books/NBK361929/ doi: 10.1596/978-1-4648-0426-7_ch12

Lewchuk,W., de Wolff, A., King, A., &Polyani, M. (2003). From Job Strain to Precarious Employment: Health Effects of Precarious Employment. *Just Labour,3*, 24.

Levesque, J.-F., Harris, M. F., & Russell, G. (2013). Patientcentred access to health care: conceptualising access at the interface of health systems and populations. *International Journal for Equity in Health, 12*, 18. doi. org/10.1186/1475-9276-12-18

Levin, C., &Chisholm, D. Cost-Effectiveness and Affordability of Interventions, Policies, and Platforms for the Prevention and Treatment of Mental, Neuro- logical, and Substance Use Disorders. In: Patel V, Chisholm D, Dua T, et al., (eds.). Mental, Neurological, and Substance Use Disorders: Disease Control Priorities, Third Edition (Volume 4). Washington (DC): The International Bank for Reconstruction and Development / The World Bank; 2016 Mar 14. Chapter 12. Available from: https://www.ncbi.nlm.nih.gov/books/NBK361929/ doi: 10.1596/978-1-4648-0426-7_ch12

Lewchuk,W., de Wolff, A., King, A., &Polyani, M. (2003). From Job Strain to Precarious Employment: Health Effects of Precarious Employment. *Just Labour,3*, 24

Lewis, G., & Booth, M. (1992). Regional differences in mental health in Great Britain. *Journal of epidemiology and community health, 46*(6), 608-11

Link, B. G., & Phelan, J. (1995). Social Conditions as Fundamental Causes of Disease. *Journal of Health & Social Behavior, 35*(Extra Issue), 80–94. doi:10.2307/2626958

Liu, J., MA, H., HE, Y.-L., XIE, B., XU, Y.-F., TANG, H.-Y., YU, X. (2011). Mental health system in China: history, recent service reform and future challenges. *World Psychiatry, 10*(3), 210–216.

Livingstone S, Smith PK(2014). Annual research review: Harms experienced by child users of online and mobile technologies: the nature, prevalence and management of sexual and aggressive risks in the digital age. J Child Psychol Psychiatry. 2014;55:635–54. 10.1111/jcpp.12197

Lloyd, C., Waghorn, G., &Williams, P. L. (2008). Conceptualising recovery in mental health rehabilitation. *British Journal of Occupational Therapy, 71*(8), 321-328.

Lorant, V., Deliège, D., Eaton, W., Robert, A., Philippot, P., &Ansseau, M. (2003). Socioeconomic inequalities in depression: a meta-analysis. *Am J Epidemiol,15*, 157(2), 98-112.

Lodovici, M. S., &Semenza,R.(ed.) (2012). Precarious work and high-Skilled youth in Europe.

Lonnie, G. (2012). The effects of working time on productivity and firm perfor- mance: a research synthesis paper/ prepared by Lonnie Golden ; International Labour Office, Conditions of Work and Employment Branch. - Geneva: ILO.

Lund, C., Breen, A., Flisher, A. J., Kakuma, R., Corrigall, J., Joska, J. A., ... Patel, V. (2010). Poverty and common mental disorders in low and middle income countries: A systematic review. *Social Science & Medicine (1982), 71*(3), 517–528.

Lund, C., Tomlinson, M., De Silva, M., Fekadu, A., Shidhaye, R., Jordans, M., ... Patel, V. (2012). PRIME: A programme to reduce the treatment gap for mental disorders in five low- and middle-income countries. *PLoS Med, 9*,e1001359.

Lund, C., Brooke-Sumner, C., Baingana, F., Baron, E. C., Breuer, E., Chandra, P., ... Saxena,S. (2018).Social determinants of mental disorders and the Sustainable Development Goals: a systematic review of reviews. *Lancet Psychiatry, 5*(4), 357-369.

Luthar, S. S., & D'avanzo, K. (1999). Contextual factors in substance use: A study of suburbanand inner-city adolescents. *Development and Psychopathology, 11*(4), 845–867.

Lynch, J., Smith, G. D., Harper, S., Hillemeier, M., Ross, N., Kaplan, G. A., & Wolfson, M. (2004). Is income inequality a determinant of population health? Part 1. A systematic review. *The Milbank quarterly, 82*(1), 5–99. doi:10.1111/j.0887-378X.2004.00302.x

Lynch, J., & Kaplan, G.(2000). Socioeconomic position. In L. Berkman& I. Kawachi (Eds.) *Social Epidemiology.* New York: Oxford University Press.

MTF (2018): NATIONAL SURVEY RESULTS ON DRUG USE 2017 Overview Key Findings on Adolescent Drug Use

Macinko, James A., Leiyu Shi, Barbara Starfield, and John T. Wulu. 2003. "Income Inequality and Health: A Critical Review of the Literature." Medical Care Research and Review 60(4):407–52.

Mackenzie, C. S., Gekoski, W. L., &Knox, V. J. (2006). Age, gender, and the underutilization of mental health services: the influence of help-seeking attitudes. *Aging Ment Health,See comment in PubMed Commons below10*(6), 574-82.

Mann, C. J. (2003).Observational research methods. Research design II: cohort, cross sectional, and case-control studies. *Emerg Med J, 20*, 54–60.

Marmot MG.(1999) Job insecurity in a broader social and health context; Labour market changes and job insecurity: A challenge for social welfare and health promotion. WHO Reg Publ Eur Ser. 1999;81:1–9.

Marmot M, Wilkinson R, editors. , editors(2003): *Social determinants of health: the solid facts.* 2nd ed. Copenhagen (Denmark): World Health Organization Regional Office for Europe; 2003.

Marmot M, Wilkinson RG. Psychosocial and material pathways in the relation between income and health: a response to Lynch et al. *BMJ.* 2001 May 19;322(7296):1233-6. doi: 10.1136/bmj.322.7296.1233. PMID: 11358781; PMCID: PMC1120336.

Marmot, M. (2005).Social determinants of health inequalities. *The Lancet, 365*,1099–1104.

Mamot, M. (2007).Achieving health equity: from root causes to fair outcomes, *Lancet, 370*: 1153–63

Marmot, M. (2010). The Marmot Review Fair Society, Healthy Lives: Strategic Review of Health Inequalities in England post-2010, February 2010.

Marmot, M. (2014b). Book Capital Health, Perspectives.*Lancet, 384*, 394-395.

Marmot, M., Allen, J., Bell, R., Bloomer, E., &Goldblatt, P. (2012). WHO European review of social determinants of health and the health divide. *The Lancet, 380*(9846), 1011-1029.

Marmot, M.,& Bell, R. (2012). Fair Society, health lives.*Public Health, 126*(Sup- plement 1), S4-S10.

Marmot, M.,& Brunner, E. (2005b). Cohort Profile: The Whitehall II study. *International Journal of Epidemiology, 34*, 251–256.

Marmot, M. G., Griffiths, J., Ziglio, E. (Eds.).(1999). Labour market changes and job insecurity: A challenge for social welfare and health promotion Copenhagen: WHO Regional Publications, European Series, No 81.

Marmot, M. G., Smith, G. D., Stansfield, S., Patel, C., Fiona, N., Head, J., …Feeney, A. (1991). Health inequality among British civil servants: The Whitehall II study. *The Lancet, 337*(8):1387–1393.

The Marmot Review (2010). Fair Society, Healthy Lives: Strategic Review of Health Inequalities in England post-2010, February 2010. UCL Institute of Health Equity. http://www.parliament.uk/documents/fair-society-healthy- lives-full-report.pd

Marmot, M. (2014a). Commentary: Mental health and public health.*Interna- tional Journal of Epidemiology*, 293–296.

Mateus, M. D., Mari, J. J., Delgado, P. G., Almeida-Filho, N., Barrett, T., Gerolin, J., … Saxena, S. (2008). The mental health system in Brazil: Policies and future challenges. *International Journal of Mental Health Systems, 2*, 12.

Mathers C. D. (2011). Global burden of disease in young people aged 10-24 years: a systematic analysis. *LANCET,377*(9783), 2093 – 2102.

McDaid, D., Knapp, M., &Raja, S. (2008). Barriers in the mind: promoting an economic case for mental health in low- and middle-income countries. *World Psychiatry, 7*(2), 79–86.

McKee, M. (1999). Alcoholism in Russia, Alcohol and Alcoholism,34(6), 824–829. McLeod, C. B., Lavis, J. N., Mustard, C. A., &Stoddart, G. L. (2003). Income Inequality, Household Income, and Health Status in Canada: A Prospective Cohort Study. *American Journal of Public Health, 93*(8), 1287–1293.

McLellan A. T. (2017). Substance Misuse and Substance use Disorders: Why do they Matter in Healthcare?. *Transactions of the American Clinical and Climatological Association, 128*, 112-130.

Medeiros, H., McDaid, D., Knapp, M.,&The Mheen Group. (2008). Shifting Care from Hospital to the Community in Europe: Economic Challenges and Opportunities(accessed March 22, 2016). Retrieved from http://www. researchgate.net/publication/30524181_ Shifting_care_from_hospital_to_ the_community_in_Europe_economic_challenges_and_opportunities

Mehrotra, A., Forrest, C. B., & Lin, C. Y. (2011). Dropping the Baton: Specialty Referrals in the United States. *The Milbank Quarterly, 89*(1), 39–68.

Mental Health Commission of Canada. (2013a). *Opening Minds, Interim Report* (accessed March 22, 2016

Mental Health Commission of Canada. (2013b). *School-Based Mental Health in Canada: A Final Report, School-Based Mental Health and Substance Abuse Consortium* (accessed March 22, 2016). Retrieved from https:// www.mentalhealthcommission.ca/English/system/files/ private/document/ ChildYouth_School_Based_Mental_Health_ Canada_Final_Report_ENG. pdf

Mental Health commission of Canada (2014): Toronto Final Report (At Home/Chez Soi Project)

Mental Health Commission of Canada. (2015). *Informing the Future: Mental Health Indicators for Canada, Ottawa* (accessed March 22, 2016). Retrieved from http://www.mentalhealthcommission.ca/

English/system/files/private/ document/MHCC_MentalHealthIndicators_ENG_full_June2015.pdf

Merikangas, K. R., Nakamura, E. F., &Kessler, R. C. (2009). Epidemiology of Mental Disorders in Children and Adolescents. *Dialogues in Clinical Neurosci- ence, 11*, 7–20.

Merikangas, K. R., He, J., Burstein, M., Swanson, S. A., Avenevoli, S., Cui, L., ... Swendsen, J. (2010). Lifetime Prevalence of Mental Disorders in US Adolescents: Results from the National Comorbidity Study-Adolescent Supplement (NCS-A). *Journal of the American Academy of Child and Adoles- cent Psychiatry, 49*(10), 980–989.

Merikangas, K. R., & McClair, V. L. (2012). Epidemiology of substance use disorders. *Human genetics, 131*(6), 779-89.; Degenhardt L, Chiu W-T, Sampson N, Kessler RC, Anthony JC, Angermeyer M, Bruffaerts R, de Girolamo G, Gureje O, Huang Y, Karam A, Kostyuchenko S, Lepine JP, Mora MEM, Neumark Y, Ormel JH, Pinto-Meza A, Posada-Villa J, Stein DJ, Takeshima T, Wells JE. Toward a Global View of Alcohol, Tobacco, Cannabis, and Cocaine Use: Findings from the WHO World Mental Health Surveys. PLoS Med. 2008;5(7):e141

Mirowsky, J., Ross, C. E. (1989). Social causes of psychological distress. Haw- thorne, NY: Aldine De Gruyter.

Misra, J., Moller, S., & Budig, M. J. (2007). Work Family Policies and Poverty for Partnered and Single Women in Europe and North America. *Gender and Society, 21*, 804-825.

Mojtabai, R., Olfson,M.,Sampson,N.A., Jin, R., Druss, B., Wang,P.S., ... Kessler, R. C. (2011). Barriers to Mental Health Treatment: Results from the National Comorbidity Survey Replication. *Psychological Medicine, 41,* 1751–61. doi.org/10.1017/S0033291710002291

Moilanen, I., &Rantakallio, P. (1988). The single parent family and child's mental health. *Soc Sci Med,27*, 181-6.

Morris, J., Lora, A., McBain, R., &Saxena, S. (2012). Global Mental Health Resources and Services: A WHO Survey of 184 Countries.*Public Health Reviews, 34*, 1–19 (accessed March 22, 2016). Retrieved from http://www. publichealthreviews.eu/upload/pdf_files/12/00_Morris.pdf

Moscone, F., Tosetti, E., &Vittadini, G.(2016). The impact of precarious employ- ment on mental health: The case of Italy. *Social Science & Medicine, 158*, 86-95.

Moussavi S, Chatterji S, Verdes E, Tandon A, Patel V, & Ustun B (2007). Depression, chronic diseases, and decrements in health: results from the World Health Surveys. *The Lancet, 370*(9590), 851–858.

Mrazek PB, Haggerty RJ. (1994): Reducing Risks for Mental Disorders: Frontiers for Preventive Intervention Research. National Academy of Sciences. 1994.

Mueser, Kim T., Gary R. Bond, Robert E. Drake, and Sandra G. Resnick. 1998. Models of Community Care for Severe Mental Illness: A Review of Research on Case Management. *Schizophrenia Bulletin, 24*, 37–74. doi:10.1093/ oxfordjournals.schbul.a033314

Muntaner, C., Eaton, W. W.,Miech, R., &O'Campo, P. (2004). Socioeconomic Position and Major Mental Disorders.*Epidemiologic Reviews, 26*, 53–62.

Murali, V.,&Oyebode, F. (2004). Poverty, social inequality and mental health. *Advances in Psychiatric Treatment, 10*, 216-224.

National Collaborating Centre for Mental Health (UK)(2011) . Common Mental Health Disorders: Identification and Pathways to Care. Leicester (UK): British Psychological Society; 2011. (NICE Clinical Guidelines, No. 123.) 2, COMMON MENTAL HEALTH DISORDERS.

National Health Service. (2010). "Collaborative Care, Primary Care Commis- sioning" (accessed March 22, 2016). Retrieved from http://www.iapt.nhs.uk/ silo/files/collaborative-care-report--phase-1--june-2010.pdf

National Institute on Drug Abuse (NIDA)(2018) : Common Comorbidities with Substance Use Disorders Last Updated February

2018

NIDA. (2018, August 1). Comorbidity: Substance Use Disorders and Other Mental Illnesses. Retrieved from

National Research Council and Institute of Medicine. (2009). Preventing Mental, Emotional, and Behavioral Disorders Among Young People: Progress and Possibilities. Washington, DC: The National Academies Press. doi. org/10.17226/12480

National Survey on Drug Use and Health (2014): Summary of National Find- ings, NSDUH Series H-48, HHS Publication No. (SMA) 14-4863.

Ngui, E.M., Khasakhala, L.,Ndetei, D.,&Roberts, L. W. (2010). Mental Dis- orders, Health Inequalities and Ethics: A Global Perspective.*International Review of Psychiatry, 22*, 235–44.

National Institute on Drug Abuse (NIDA). (2010). Comorbidity: Addiction and Other Mental Illnesses.

NIDA. (2017, March 23). Health Consequences of Drug Misuse. Retrieved from Retrieved from https://www.drugabuse.gov/related-topics/health-consequences-drug-misuse

NIDA. (2018, August 1). Comorbidity: Substance Use Disorders and Other Mental Illnesses.

O'Brien, S., McFarland, J., Kealy, B., Pullela, A., Saunders, J., Cullen, W., Mea- gher, D.(2012). A randomized-controlled trial of intensive case management emphasizing the recovery model among patients with severe and enduring mental illness. *Ir J Med Sci ,181*(3), 301-8.

O'Dea, B., Glozier, N., Purcell, R., McGorry, P. D., Scott, J., Feilds, K.-L., … Hickie, I. B. (2014). A cross-sectional exploration of the clinical characteris- tics of disengaged (NEET) young people in primary mental healthcare. *BMJ Open, 4*(12), e006378.

Office of the Surgeon General (US). (2001). Center for Mental Health Services (US); National Institute of Mental Health (US). Mental Health: Culture, Race, and Ethnicity: A Supplement to Mental Health: A Report of the Sur- geon General. Rockville (MD): Substance Abuse and Mental Health Services Administration (US); 2001 Aug. Chapter 7 A Vision for the Future.

Olesen, S., Butterworth, P., Leach, L., &Pirkis, K.J. 2013. Mental health affects future employment as job loss affects mental health: Findings from a longitudinal population study.*BMC Psychiatry, 13*, 144.

Organisation for Economic Co-operation and Development (OECD). (2008a). *Mental Health in OECD Countries. Policy Brief.* OECD Publishing.

Organisation for Economic Co-operation and Development (OECD). (2008b). *Employment Outlook 2008.* OECD Publishing.

Organisation for Economic Co-operation and Development (OECD). (2008c). Growing Unequal? Income Distribution and Poverty in OECD Countries. Paris: OECD.

Organisation for Economic Co-operation and Development (OECD). (2009). *In-Work Poverty: What Can Governments Do? Policy Brief.*Retrieved from https://www.oecd.org/els/43650040.pdf

Organisation for Economic Co-operation and Development (OECD). (2010). Tackling Inequalities in Brazil, China, India and South Africa: The Role of Labour Market and Social Policies.OECD Publishing

Organisation for Economic Co-operation and Development (OECD). (2011a). Health at a Glance. OECD Indicators. OECD Publishing.

Organisation for Economic Co-operation and Development (OECD). (2011b). Divided we stand – why inequality keeps rising

Organisation for Economic Co-operation and Development (OECD). (2011c): Doing Better for Families, Ch 1. Retrieved from https://www.oecd.org/els/ soc/47701118.pdf

Organisation for Economic Co-operation and Development (OECD). (2012). *Sick on the Job? Myths and Realities about Mental*

Health and Work. OECD Publishing.

Organisation for Economic Co-operation and Development (OECD).(2013).The Challenge of Inequality: Time For Change.

Organisation for Economic Co-operation and Development (OECD). (2014a). *Making Mental Health Count: The Social and Economic Costs of Neglecting Mental Health Care*(accessed March 22, 2016). Retrieved fromhttp://www. keepeek.com/Digital-Asset-Management/oecd/social-issues-migration-health/ making-mental-health-count_9789264208445-en#page1

Organisation for Economic Co-operation and Development (OECD). (2014b). Report of the OECD framework for Inclusive Growth.Retrieved from https://www.oecd.org/mcm/IG_MCM_ENG.pdf

Organisation for Economic Co-operation and Development (OECD). (2015a). *Global Employment Outlook 2015a.* OECD Publishing.

Organisation for Economic Co-operation and Development (OECD). (2015b). *In It Together: Why Less Inequality Benefits All.* OECD Publishing.

Organisation for Economic Co-operation and Development (OECD). (2015c).: How's Life? 2015,Measuring Well-Being

Organisation for Economic Co-operation and Development (OECD). (2015d). Fit Mind, Fit Job: From Evidence to Practice in Mental Health and Work, Mental Health and Work.Paris: OECD Publishing.

Organisation for Economic Co-operation and Development (OECD). (2016). Building More Resilient and Inclusive Labour Markets, Issues Paper, OECD Labour and Employment Ministerial Meeting 15 Jan. Retrieved from http:// www.oecd.org/employment/ministerial/documentation/Issues-Paper-ENG. pdf

Organisation for Economic Co-operation and Development (OECD). (2016b). Health at glance: Asia-Pacific 2016

Organisation for Economic Co-operation and Development (OECD).(2017). Understanding The Socio-economic Divide in Europe

OECD(2018): Emotional Well-being of Children and Adolescents: Recent trends and Relevant factors OECD Education Working Paper No. 169

Ormel J, VonKorff M, Ustun TB, Pini S, Korten A, Oldehinkel T(1994).

Common mental disorders and disability across cultures. Results from the WHO Collaborative Study on Psychological Problems in General Health Care. JAMA. 1994;272(22):1741–8. Epub 1994/12/14.

Ostry, J. D., Berg, A., & Tsangarides, C. G. (2014). Redistribution, Inequal- ity, and Growth. International Monetary Fund Staff Discussion Note SDN/14/02.

Paschall, M. J., Grube, J. W., & Kypri, K. (2009). Alcohol Control Policies and Alcohol Consumption by Youth: A Multi-National Study. *Addiction (Abing- don, England), 104*(11), 1849–1855.

Patel. V., Flisher, A. J., Hetrick, S., &McGorry, P. (2007). Mental health of young people: a global public-health challenge. *Lancet, 369*(9569), 1302-13.

Patel. V., Araya, R., de Lima, M., Ludermir, A., Todd, C. (1999). Women, poverty and common mental disorders in four restructuring societies. *Soc Sci Med, 49*(11), 1461-71.

Patel, V. (2007).Mental health in low- and middle-income countries.*British Medical Bulletin, 81/82,* 81–96.

Patel, V., Belkin, G. S., Chockalingam, A., Cooper, J.,Saxena, S., &Unützer, J. (2013a). Grand Challenges: Integrating Mental Health Services into Priority Health Care Platforms. *PLOS Medicine, 10,* e1001448. doi:10.1371/journal. pmed.1001448

Patel, V., Kieling, C., Maulik, P. K., & Divan, G. (2013b). Improving Access To Care For Children With Mental Disorders: A Global

Perspective. *Archives of Disease in Childhood, 98*(5), 323–327.

Patel, V., Maj, M., Flisher, A. J., De Silva, M. J., Koschorke, M., Prince, M.,WPA Zonal, &Member Society Representatives. (2010). Reducing the Treatment Gap for Mental Disorders: A WPA Survey. *World Psychiatry, 9,* 169–76. doi:10.1002/j.2051-5545.2010.tb00305.x

Patel, V., Araya, R., Chatterjee, S., Chisholm, D., Cohen, A., De Silva, M., ... van Ommeren, M. (2007).Treatment and Prevention of Mental Disorders in Low-Income and Middle-Income Countries. *Lancet,370*(9591), 991-1005.

Patel, V., Maj, M., Flisher, A. J., De Silva, M. J., Koschorke, M., Prince, M., ... Richardson, G. (2010). Reducing the treatment gap for mental disorders: a WPA survey. *World Psychiatry, 9*(3), 169–176.

Patel, V., Xiao, S., Chen, H., Hanna, F., Jotheeswaran, A. T., Luo, D., ... Saxena, S. (2016). The magnitude of and health system responses to the mental health treatment gap in adults in India and China. *Lancet, 388,* 3074–3084.

Patel V, Chisholm D, Dua T, et al., editors(2016). Mental, Neurological, and Substance Use Disorders: Disease Control Priorities, Third Edition (Volume 4). Washington (DC): The International Bank for Reconstruction and Development / The World Bank; 2016 Mar 14. Disease Control Priorities

Patel, V., Burns, J. K., Dhingra, M., Tarver, L., Kohrt, B. A., & Lund, C. (2018). Income inequality and depression: a systematic review and meta-analysis of the association and a scoping review of mechanisms. *World Psychiatry, 17*(1), 76–89.

Patton, G. C., Coffey, C., Lynskey, M. T., Reid, S., Hemphill, S., Carlin, J. B., &Hall W. (2007). Trajectories of adolescent alcohol and cannabis use into young adulthood. *Addiction, 102*(4), 607–615.

Peacock A, Leung J, Larney S, Colledge S, Hickman M, Rehm J, Giovino GA, West R, Hall W, Griffiths P, Ali R, Gowing L, Marsden J, Ferrari AJ, Grebely J, Farrell M, Degenhardt L(2017). Global statistics on alcohol, tobacco and illicit drug use: 2017 status report. Addiction. 2018. May 10 10.1111/ add.14234

Pearce, N., & Davey Smith, G. (2003). Is Social Capital the Key to Inequalities in Health? *American Journal of Public Health, 93*(1), 122–129.

Penn, D. L., &Corrigan, P. W. (2002). The Effects of Stereotype Suppression on Psychiatric Stigma.*Schizophrenia Research, 55,* 269– 76. doi:10.1016/ S0920-9964(01)00207-9

Perou, R., Bitsko, R. H., Blumberg, S. J., Pastor, P., Ghandour, R. M., Gfroerer, J. C., … Huang, L. N. (2013). Mental Health Surveillance among Children, United States, 2005–2011.*Morbidity and Mortality Weekly Report, 62*(Suppl), 1–35.

Perrino, T., Beardslee, W., Bernal, G., Brincks, A., Cruden, G., Howe, G.,… Brown, C. H. (2015). Towards Scientific Equity for the Prevention of Depression and Internalizing Symptoms in Vulnerable Youth.*Prevention Science: The Official Journal of the Society for Prevention Research, 16,* 642–51.

Peters D.H., Garg A., Bloom G., Walker D.G., Brieger W.R., Rahman M.H.(2008) Poverty and access to health care in developing countries. Ann. N. Y. Acad. Sci. 2008;1136:161–171. doi: 10.1196/ annals.1425.011

Piketty, T. (2015).Property, Inequality, and Taxation: Reflections on Capital in the Twenty-First Century.68 Tax L. Rev. 631

Polanczyk GV(2013): The burden of childhood mental disorders, Eur Child Ado- lesc Psychiatry. 2013 Mar;22(3):135-7. doi: 10.1007/ s00787-013-0382-1.

Quak, E., & van de Vijsel. A. (2014).Low wages and job insecurity as a destructive global standard. November 26, 2014, The Broker, Connecting the world of knowledge (Ostry , Berg,… 2014, IMF)

Quinlan, M. (2015).The effects of non-standard forms of employment on worker health and safety. Conditions of Work and Employment Series No. 67 ILO

Raphael, D. (2002).Poverty, income inequality and Health in

Canada, The CSJ Foundation for Research and Education.

Raubenheimer, J. E. (2004). An item selection procedure to maximize scale reliability and validity. *South African Journal of Industrial Psychology, 30* (4), 59-64

Rehm, J., Mathers, C., Popova, S., Thavorncharoensap, M., Teerawattananon, Y., &Patra, J. (2009). Global burden of disease and injury and economic cost attributable to alcohol use and alcohol-use disorders. *Lancet, 373*, 2223-33.

Reeves, W. C., Strine, T. W., Pratt, L. A., Thompson, W., Ahluwalia, I., Dhingra, S. S., … Safran, M. A.(2011). Mental Illness Surveillance among Adults in the United States.*Morbidity and Mortality Weekly Report, 60*, 1–29.

Regier, D. A., Farmer, M. E., Rae, D. S., Locke, B. Z., Keith, S. J., Judd, L. L.,… Goodwin, F. K. (1990). Comorbidity of mental disorders with alcohol and other drug abuse. Results from the Epidemiologic Catchment Area (ECA) Study. *JAMA, 264*(19), 2511-2518.

Reijneveld, S. A., & Schene, A. H. (1998). Higher prevalence of mental disorders in socioeconomically deprived urban areas in The Netherlands: community or personal disadvantage?. *Journal of epidemiology and community health, 52*(1), 2-7

Reiss, F. (2013). Socioeconomic inequalities and mental health problems in children and adolescents: A systematic review. *Social Science Medicine,90*, 24–31.

Rodgers, G. (1989). Precarious Work in Western Europe. In G. Rodgers and J. Rodgers (eds), *Precarious Jobs in Labour Market Regulation: The Growth of Atypical Employment in Western Europe* (pp.1-16). Belgium: International Institute for Labour Studies.

Rössler, W. (2006). Psychiatric rehabilitation today: an overview. *World Psychiatry, 5*(3), 151–157.

Rowan, K., McAlpine, D., & Blewett, L. (2013). Access and Cost Barriers to Mental Health Care by Insurance Status, 1999 to 2010. *Health Affairs (Project Hope), 32*(10), 1723–1730. doi.org/10.1377/hlthaff.2013.0133

Rowlingson, K. (2011).Does income inequality cause health and social problems? London: Joseph Rowntree Foundation.

Russell, L. (2010).Mental Health Care Services In Primary Care Tackling the Issues in the Context of Health Care, Centre for American Progress. Retrieved fromhttps://www.americanprogress.org/wp-content/uploads/ issues/2010/10/pdf/mentalhealth.pdf

Salvo, N., Bennett, K., Cheung, A., Chen, Y., Rice, M., Rush, B., … and Evidence on Tap Concurrent Disorders Collaborative Team. (2012). Prevention of Substance Use in Children/Adolescents with Mental Disorders: A Systematic Review. *Journal of the Canadian Academy of Child and Adolescent Psychiatry, 21*(4), 245–252.

SAMHSA. (2015).Center for Behavioral Health Statistics and Quality, National Survey on Drug Use and Health, 2014 and 2015.

Sanderson, K., &Andrews, G. (2006). Common Mental Disorders in the Work- force: Recent Findings from Descriptive and *Social Epidemiology.Canadian Journal of Psychiatry, 51*, 63–75.

Sanmartin, C., Hennessy, D., Lu, Y.,&Law, M. R. (2014). *Trends in Out-of-Pocket Health Care Expenditures in Canada, by Household Income, 1997 to 2009.* Ottawa: Statistics Canada.

Saraceno, B., &Saxena, S. (2005a). Mental Health Services in Central and Eastern Europe: Current State and Continuing Concerns. *Epidemiologia e Psichiatria Sociale, 14*, 44–8. doi:10.1017/S1121189X00001925

Saraceno, B., Levav, I., Kohn, R. (2005b). The public mental health significance of research onsocio-economic factors in schizophrenia and major depression. *World Psychiatry,4*, 181–185.

Sartorious N. (2013). Comorbidity of mental and physical diseases: a main challenge for medicine of the 21st century. *Shanghai archives of psychiatry, 25*(2), 68-9.

Saunders J. B., Aasland O. G., Babor T. F., De La Fuente J. R., Grant M. (1993). Development of the alcohol use disorders identification test (AUDIT): WHO collaborative project on early detection of persons with harmful alcohol consumption–II. *Addiction* 88 791–

804. 10.1111/j.1360-0443.1993. tb02093

Saunders, R. (2003). Defining Vulnerability in the Labour Market, Research Paper W|21. Ottawa: Canadian Policy Research Networks.

Sawyer, S.M., Afifi, R.A., Bearinger, L.H., Blakemore, S.J., Dick, B., Ezay, A., Patton, G.C. (2012). Adolescence: A Foundation for Future Health. *Lancet, 379*, 1630–1640.

Saxena, S., Llopis, E. J., & Hosman, C. (2006): Prevention of mental and behavioural disorders: implications for policy and practice. *World Psychiatry,* 5(1), 5–14.

Saxena, S., Thornicroft, G., Knapp, M., &White ford, H. (2007). Resources for Mental Health: Scarcity, Inequity, and Inefficiency.*Lancet, 370*, 878–89.

Semrau, M., Evans-Lacko, S., Alem, A., Ayuso-Mateos, J. L., Chisholm, D., Gureje, O., ... Thornicroft, G.(2015). Strengthening mental health systems in low- and middle-income

Sen, A. K. (1993).Capability and Well-being. in Martha C. Nussbaum and Amartya K. Sen (Eds.), *The Quality of Life,* (pp. 30-53). Oxford: Clarendon Press

Sen, A. K. (1994).Well-Being, Capability and Public Policy. *Giornale DelgiEcono- mist e Annali di Economia*, 53, 333-47.

Sen, A. (2001), *Development as Freedom*. New York: Alfred A. Knopf.

Schoen, C., Osborn, R., Squires, D.,&Doty, M. M. (2013).Access, Affordability, and Insurance Complexity Are Often Worse in the United States Compared to 10 Other Countries," *Health Affairs*

Schulte, M. T., & Hser, Y. I. (2014). Substance Use and Associated Health Conditions throughout the Lifespan. *Public health reviews,* 35(2), https:// web-beta.archive.org/web/20150206061220/http:// www.publichealthre- views.eu/upload/pdf_files/14/00_Schulte_Hser.pdf.

Scott, H. K. (2004). Reconceptualizing the nature and health consequences of work-related insecurity for the new economy: the decline of workers' power in the flexibility regime. *Int J Health Serv, 34,* 143–53.

Scruggs, L., &Allan, J. (2006). Welfare-State Decommodification in Eighteen OECD Countries: A Replication and Revision.*Journal of European Social Policy,16,* 55–72.

Schroeder, S. A. (2012). Incidence, prevalence, and hybrid approaches to calculating disability-adjusted life years. *Population Health Metrics, 10,* 19. doi.org/10.1186/1478-7954-10-19

Seal K.H., Bertenthal D., Miner C.R., Sen S., Marmar C.R(2007). Mental health disorders among 103,788 US veterans returning from Iraq and Afghanistan seen at Department of Veterans Affairs facilities. Arch. Intern. Med. 2007;167:476–482. doi: 10.1001/archinte.167.5.476.

Sharpe, M., Walker, J., Hansen, C. H., Martin, P., Symeonides, S., Gourley, C., ... Murray, G. (2014). Integrated Collaborative Care for Comorbid Major Depression in Patients with Cancer (SMaRT Oncology-2): A Multicentre Randomised Controlled Effectiveness Trial. *Lancet, 384,* 1099–108. doi:10.1016/S0140-6736(14)61231-9

Shek, O.,Pietila, I.,Graeser, S.,& Aarva, P. (2010). Redesigning mental health policy in PostSoviet Russia: A qualitative analysis of health policy documents (1992–2006). *International Journal of Mental Health, 39*(4), 16–39.

Shim, R., Koplan, C., Langheim, F., Manseau, M., Powers, R., Compton, M. (2014). The Social Determinants of Mental Health: An Overview and Call to Action. *Psychiatr Ann,44,*22-26. doi:10.3928/00485713-20140108-04

Shinn, M., Gibbons-Benton, J., & Brown, S. R. (2015). Poverty, Homelessness, and Family Break-Up. *Child Welfare, 94*(1), 105–122.

Shonkoff JP, Garner AS(2012); American Academy of Pediatrics Committee on Psychosocial Aspects of Child and Family Health; Committee on Early Childhood, Adoption, and Dependent Care;

Section on Developmental and Behavioral Pediatrics. The lifelong effects of early childhood adversity and toxic stress. Pediatrics. 2012;129(1):e232– e246.

Sienkiewicz, D. (2010). Access to Health Services in Europe European Public Health Alliance.

Skoog I(2011) Psychiatric disorders in the elderly. Can. J. Psychiatry. 2011;56:387–397.

Simmons, M., Hetrick, S., &Jorm, A. F. (2011). Experiences of Treatment Decision Making for Young People Diagnosed with Depressive Disorders: A Qualitative Study in Primary Care and Specialist Mental Health Settings. *BMC Psychiatry, 11*, 194. doi:10.1186/1471-244X-11-194

Smith, J. P. (1999). Healthy Bodies and Thick Wallets: The Dual Relation Between Health and Economic Status. *The Journal of Economic Perspectives : A Journal of the American Economic Association, 13*(2), 144–166.

Smith, C.P. & Freyd, J.J. (2013). Dangerous Safe Havens: Institutional Betrayal Exacerbates Sexual Trauma. *Journal of Traumatic Stress, 26*, 119-124.

Smith, C.P. & Freyd, J.J. (2014). Institutional Betrayal. *American Pschologist, 69*(6), 575-587.

Smith. C.P. (2016). First, Do No Harm: Institutional Betrayal in Health care, PH.D dissertation submitted to the Department of Psychology and the Graduate School of the University of Oregon Social Care, Local Government and Care Partnership Directorate, UK Department of Health. 2014. "Closing the Gap: Priorities for Essential Change in Mental Health." Mental Health Partnerships. Retrieved from http://mentalhealthpartnerships.com/ resource/closing-the-gap/

Social Exclusion Unit. (2004). *Mental Health and Social Exclusion.* London: Office of the Deputy Prime Minister.

Solar, O., &Irwin, A. (2007). *Towards a conceptual framework for analysis and action on the social determinants of health.* WHO, Commission on Social Determinants of Health.

Solow, R. M.(2014).Thomas Piketty Is Right Everything you need to know about 'Capital in the Twenty-First Century.

Starfield, B., Shi, L., & Macinko, J. (2005). Contribution of Primary Care to Health Systems and Health. *The Milbank Quarterly, 83*(3), 457–502. doi. org/10.1111/j.1468-0009.2005.00409.x

Steel, Z., Marnane, C., Iranpour, C., Chey, T., Jackson, J. W., Patel, V., &Silove, D. (2014). The global prevalence of common mental disorders: a systematic review and meta-analysis 1980–2013. International Journal of Epidemiology, 43(2), 476–493.

Stiglitz, J. (2016). Inequality and Economic Growth. Political Quarterly, July 2016 https://doi.org/10.1111/1467-923X.12237

Strong, V., Waters, R.,Hibberd, C., Murray, G., Wall, L., Walker, J., ... Sharpe, M. (2008). Management of Depression for People with Cancer (SMaRT oncology 1): A Randomised Trial.*Lancet, 372*, 40–8. doi:10.1016/ S0140-6736(08)60991-5

Strohle, A. (2009). Physical activity, exercise, depression and anxiety disorders. *J Neural Transm (Vienna), 116*(6), 777–84.

Substance Abuse and Mental Health Services Administration (SAMHSA). (2012). Results from the 2011 National Survey on Drug Use and Health: Mental Health Findings. Series H-45, HHS Publication No. 12-4725. Rockville, MD: Substance Abuse and Mental Health Services Administration Center for Behavioral Health Statistics and Quality.

Substance Abuse and Mental Health Services Administration (SAMHSA). (2013). Results from the 2012 National Survey on Drug Use and Health: Summary of National Findings, (accessed March 17, 2016). Retrieved from http:// archive.samhsa.gov/data/NSDUH/2012SummNatFindDetTables/Index.aspx.

Substance Abuse and Mental Health Services Administration (SAMHSA). (2014). Results from the 2013 National Survey on Drug Use and Health: Mental Health Findings. Series H-49, HHS Publication No. 14-4887. Rockville, MD: Substance Abuse and Mental

Health Services Administration Center for Behavioral Health Statistics and Quality.

Substance Abuse and Mental Health Services Administration. (2017). Key substance use and mental health indicators in the United States: Results from the 2016 National Survey on Drug Use and Health.

Summers, L.H. (2015).Demand Side Secular Stagnation. *American Economic Review: Papers and Proceedings, 105*(5), 60-65.

Summers L H (2016): The Age of Secular Stagnation: What It Is and What to Do About It Foreign Affairs February 15, 2016

Sverke, M., Hellgren, J.,& Näswall, K. (2002).No security: a meta-analysis and review of job insecurity and its consequences. *Journal of Occupational Health Psychology,7*(3), 242–264.

Sweetland, A. C., Oquendo, M. A., Sidat, M.,Santos, P. F., Vermund, S. H., Duarte, C. S., … Wainberg, M. L. (2014). Closing the Mental Health Gap in Low-Income Settings by Building Research Capacity: Perspectives from Mozambique.*Annals of Global Health, 80,* 126–33. doi:10.1016/j. aogh.2014.04.014

Tang, N., Stein, J., Hsia, R. Y., Maselli, J. H., &Gonzales, R. (2010). Trends and Characteristics of U.S. Emergency Department Visits, 1997–2007." JAMA, 304, 664–70. doi:10.1001/jama.2010.1112

THE 2015 ESPAD REPORT: Results from the European School Survey Project on Alcohol and Other Drugs

Thombs, B. D., Roseman, M.,&Kloda, L. A. (2012). Depression Screening and Mental Health Outcomes in Children and Adolescents: A Systematic Review Protocol.*Systematic Reviews, 1,* 58. doi:10.1186/2046-4053-1-58

Thornicroft, G., & Tansella, M. (2004). Components of a Modern Mental Health Service: A Pragmatic Balance of Community and Hospital Care: Overview of Systematic Evidence.British Journal of Psychiatry: The Journal of Mental Science, 185, 283–90. doi:10.1192/bjp.185.4.283

Thornicroft, G. (2008). Stigma and discrimination limit access to mental health care. Epidemiol Psichiatr Soc, 17(1), 14–19.

Thornicroft, G., &Tansella, M. (2009).*Better mental health care.* Cambridge: Cambridge University Press.

Thornicroft, G., Cooper, S., Van Bortel, T., Kakuma, R., &Lund, C. (2012). Capacity Building in Global Mental Health Research." *Harvard Review of Psychiatry, 20,* 13–24. doi:10.3109/10673229.201 2.649117

Thornicroft, G., Deb, T., & Henderson, C. (2016). Community mental health care worldwide: current status and further developments. *World Psychiatry, 15*(3), 276–286.

Thota, A. B, Sipe, T. A., Byard, G. J., Zometa, C. S., Hahn, R. A., McK- night-Eily, L. R., ... Community Preventive Service Task Force. (2012).Collaborative Care to Improve the Management of Depressive Disorders: A Community Guide Systematic Review and Meta-Analysis." *American Journal of Preventive Medicine,42*(5), 525–38. doi:10.1016/j.amepre.2012.01.019

Tiihonen, J., Isohanni, M., Räsänen, P., Koiranen, M., &Moring, J. (1997).

Specific major mental disorders and criminality: A 26-year prospective study of the 1966 Northern Finland birth cohort. *American Journal of Psychiatry, 154*(6), 840-845

Tobias, M., Gerritsen, S., Kokaua, J., &Templeton, R. (2009). Psychiatric illnes among a nationally representative sample of sole and partnered parents in New Zealand. *Australian and New Zealand Journal of Psychiatry 43*(2), 136–144.

Tobias, R. D. (2016).An Introduction to Partial Least Squares Regression, SAS Institute Inc., Cary, NC. Retrieved from https://stats.idre.ucla.edu/wp-con- tent/uploads/2016/02/pls.pdf

Trautmann, S., Rehm, J., & Wittchen, H. U. (2016). The economic costs of mental disorders: Do our societies react appropriately to the burden of mental disorders?. *EMBO reports, 17*(9), 1245-9.

Toronto Public Health (2018): Discussion Paper: A Public Approach to Drugs.

Toumbourou JW, Stockwell T, Neighbors C, Marlatt GA, Sturge J, Rehm J.(2007) Interventions to reduce harm associated with adolescent substance use. Lancet. 2007;369:1391–1401. doi: 10.1016/S0140-6736(07)60369-9.

Tyrer, P., &Simmonds, S. (2003). Treatment Models for Those with Severe Mental Illness and Comorbid Personality Disorder." *British Journal of Psychiatry,182*, S15–8. doi:10.1192/bjp.182.44.s15

UN ESCAP. (2014a).Youth and Mental Health in Asia-Pacific, Announce- ments. Retrieved from https://www.unescap.org/announcement/ youth-and-mental-health-asia-pacific

UN ESCAP. (2014b). Youth and Mental Health in Asia-Pacific. Retrieved from https://www.unescap.org/announcement/ youth-and-mental-health-asia-pacific

United Nations. (2014). Mental Health Matters: Social Inclusion of Youth with Mental Health Conditions. Division for Social Policy and Development Department of Economic and Social Affairs. New York: United Nations.

United Nations. (2016). Leaving no one behind: the imperative of inclusive development, Report on the World Social Situation 2016, Ch 2.

UNODC(2009) World Drug Report 2009

UNODC(2018, Vol 4): DRUGS AND AGE Drugs and associated issues among young people and older people

US Preventive Services Task Force. (2009). Screening and Treatment for Major Depressive Disorder in Children and Adolescents: U.S. Preventive Services Task Force Recommendation Statement. *Pediatrics, 123*, 1223–8. doi:10.1542/peds.2008-2381

Unützer, J. (2013). The Collaborative Care Model: An Approach for Integrating Physical and Mental Health Care in Medicaid Health Homes.

Üstün, T.B. (1999). Global Burden of Mental Disorders." *American Journal of Public Health, 89*,1315–18.

Van de Werfhorst, H. G., &Salverda, W. G. (2012). Consequences of Economic Inequality: Introduction to a Special Issue. *Research in Social Stratification and Mobility, 30*(4), 377-387.

Van Ginneken, N., Jain, S., Patel, V., & Berridge, V. (2014). The development of mental health services within primary care in India: learning from oral history. *International Journal of Mental Health Systems, 8*, 30. doi. org/10.1186/1752-4458-8-30

Van Oort, F. V. A., van Lenthe, F. J., &Mackenbach, J. (2005). Material, psycho- social, and behavioural factors in the explanation of educational inequalities in mortality in the Netherlands. *Journal of Epidemiology and Community Health, 59*(3), 214–220.

Vasiliadis, H. M., Lesage, A., Adair, C., Boyer, R. (2005).Service use for mental health reasons: cross-provincial differences in rates, determinants, and equity of access. *Can J Psychiatry, 50*(10),614-619.

Vega, W. A., Kolody, B., Aguilar-Gaxiola, S., & Catalano, R. (1999). Gaps in services utilization by Mexican Americans with mental health problems. *American Journal of Psychiatry, 156*, 928–934.

Vigo, D., Thornicroft, G., & Atun, R. (2016). Estimating the true global burden of mental illness. The Lancet Psychiatry, 3(2), 171–178.

Viner, R. M., Ozer, E. M., Denny, S., Marmot, M., Resnick, M., Fatusi, A., & Currie, C. (2012). Adolescence and the social determinants of health. *Lancet, 379*(9826), 1641–52. doi:10.1016/S0140-6736(12)60149-4

Virtanen, M., Kivimäki, M., Elovainio, M., Vahtera, J., Ferrie, J. E. (2003).

From insecure to secure employment: changes in work, health, health related behaviours, and sickness absence. *Occup Environ Med, 60*, 948–53.

Vives, A., Amable, M., Ferrer, M., Moncada, S., Llorens, C.,

Muntaner, C., ..., Benach, J. (2013). Employment precariousness and poor mental health: evidence from Spain on a new social determinant of health. *J Environ Public Health,3*,978656.

Waddell, C., McEwan, K., Shepherd, C. A., Offord, D. R., &Hua, J. M. (2005). A Public Health Strategy to Improve the Mental Health of Canadian Children. *Canadian Journal of Psychiatry, 50*, 226–33.

Wagstaff. A. (2002). Poverty and health sector inequalities, Bulletin of the World Health Organization,80, 97-105.

Wahl, O. F. (1999). Mental Health Consumers' Experience of Stigma. *Schizophrenia Bulletin, 25*, 467–78. doi:10.1093/oxfordjournals.schbul.a033394

Wahlbeck, K., &McDaid, D. (2012). Actions to Alleviate the Mental Health Impact of the Economic Crisis. *World Psychiatry, 11*, 139–45. doi:10.1002/j.2051-5545.2012.tb00114.x

Walsh, E., Buchanan, A.,& Fahy, T. (2002). Violence and schizophrenia: examining the evidence. *Br J Psychiatry, 180*, 490–495.

Walsh, F. P.,& Tickle, A. C. (2013). Working towards recovery: The role of employment in recovery from serious mental health problems: a qualitative meta-synthesis. *International Journal of Psychosocial Rehabilitation, 17*(2), 35-49.

Wang, P. S., Berglund, P., Olfson, M., Pincus, H. A., Wells, K. B., & Kessler, R. C. (2005). "Failure and Delay in Initial Treatment Contact after First Onset of Mental Disorders in the National Comorbidity Survey Replication." *Archives of General Psychiatry, 62*, 603–13. doi:10.1001/archpsyc.62.6.603

Wang, P. S., Aguilar-Gaxiola, S., Alonso, J., Angermeyer, M. C., Borges, G., Bromet, E. J., ... Wells, J. E. (2007a). Worldwide Use of Mental Health Services for Anxiety, Mood, and Substance Disorders: Results from 17 Countries in the WHO World Mental Health (WMH) Surveys. *Lancet, 370*(9590), 841–850. http://doi.org/10.1016/S0140-6736(07)61414-7

Wang, J. L., Lesage, A., Schmitz, N., & Drapeau, A.(2008). The relationship between work stress and mental disorders in men and women: findings from a population-based study. *Journal of Epidemiology & Community Health, 62*(1), 42.

Warren, J. R. (2009). Socio-economic Status and Health across the Life Course: A Test of the Social Causation and Health Selection Hypotheses. Soc Forces, 87(4), 2125–2153.

Weeks, J. (2005). Inequality Trends in Some Developed OECD Countries, UN DESA Working Paper No. 6ST/ESA/2005/DWP/6

Wicks-Lim, J. (2012). The Working Poor: A Booming Demographic. New Labor Forum.

WEF. (2017). The Inclusive Growth and Development Report 2017.

Wellesley Institute. (2015). Access to Prescription Drugs: HEIA in The Federal Election. Toronto: The Wellesley Institute.

Wells, K. B., Kataoka, S. H., &Asarnow, J. R. (2001). Affective Disorders in Children and Adolescents: Addressing Unmet Need in Primary Care Settings. *Biological Psychiatry, 49*, 1111–20. doi:10.1016/S0006-3223(01)01113-1

Whelan, R., Watts, R., Orr, C. A., Althoff, R. R., Artiges, E., Banaschewski, T., Barker, G. J., Bokde, A. L., Büchel, C., Carvalho, F. M., Conrod, P. J., Flor, H., Fauth-Bühler, M., Frouin, V., Gallinat, J., Gan, G., Gowland, P., Heinz, A., Ittermann, B., Lawrence, C., Mann, K., Martinot, J. L., Nees, F., Ortiz, N., Paillère-Martinot, M. L., Paus, T., Pausova, Z., Rietschel, M., Robbins,T. W., Smolka, M. N., Ströhle, A., Schumann, G., Garavan, H., IMAGEN Consortium (2014). Neuropsychosocial profiles of current and future adolescent alcohol misusers. *Nature, 512*(7513), 185-9.

White, F. (2015). Primary Health Care and Public Health: Foundations of Universal Health Systems. Med Princ Pract,24, 10.

Whitehead, M. (1992). The concepts and principles of equity and health. *Int J Health Serv,22*, 42945.

Whiteford, H. A., Ferrari, A. J., Degenhardt, L., Feigin, V., &Vos, T. (2015). The Global Burden of Mental, Neurological, and Substance Use Disorders: An Analysis from the Global Burden of Disease Study 2010.*PLoS One, 10*:e0116820. doi:10.1371/journal.pone.0116820

Whiteford, H. A., Degenhardt, L., Rehm, J.,Baxter, A. J. &Ferrari, A. J. (2013).

The Global Burden of Mental and Substance Use Disorders.*Lancet, 382,* 1575–86. doi:10.1016/S0140-6736(13)61611-6

Whiteford, H. A., Ferrari, A. J., Degenhardt, L., Feigin, V., & Vos, T.(2016). Global Burden of Mental, Neurological, and Substance Use Disorders: An Analysis from the Global Burden of Disease Study 2010. In Patel V, Chisholm D, Dua T, et al., (Eds.) Mental, Neurological, and Substance Use Disorders: Disease Control Priorities, Third Edition (Volume 4). Washington (DC): The International Bank for Reconstruction and Development / The World Bank; 2016 Mar 14. Chapter 2.

Wilkinson, R. G., &Marmot, M.(1998).*Social determinants of health. The solid facts.* Copenhagen: WHO Regional Office for Europe.

Wilkinson, R. G. (1999). Income inequality, social cohesion, and health: clarifying the theory--a reply to Muntaner and Lynch. *Int J Health Serv,29*(3), 525-43,

Wilkinson, R. G., &Pickett, K.E. (2007). The Problems of Relative Deprivation: Why Some Societies Do Better Than Others. *Social Science and Medicine, 65,* 1965–78.

Wilkinson, R.&Pickett, K. (2017).How Inequality Endangers Our Mental Health. The evidence that inequality has damaging psychological effects has now become clear. Research Commentary

Williams, D. R., Yu, Y., Jackson, J. S., & Anderson, N. B. (1997). Racial differences in physical and mental health: Socio-economic status, stress and discrimination. *Journal of Health Psychology, 2,* 335-351.

Wilson, S. J., & Lipsey, M. W. (2007). School-based interventions for aggressive and disruptive behavior: update of a meta-analysis.

American journal of preventive medicine, 33(2 Suppl), S130-43.

de Wit H. (2008). Impulsivity as a determinant and consequence of drug use: a review of underlying processes. *Addiction biology, 14*(1), 22-31.

Wittchen, H.U., Jacobi, F., Rehm, J., Gustavsson, A., Svensson, M., Jönsson, B.,...Steinhausen, H.C. (2011). The size and burden of mental disorders and other disorders of the brain in Europe 2010. *Eur. Neuropsychopharmacol.21*, 655–679.

Wold, S., Sjöström, M.,&Eriksson, L. (2001). PLS-regression: A basic tool of chemometrics.*Chemometrics and Intelligent Laboratory Systems, 58*(2),109-130.

World Health Organization. (1992). The ICD-10 Classification of Mental and Behavioural Disorders. Clinical descriptions and diagnostic guidelines.

Geneva: World Health Organization. The World Health (2002): Reducing Risks, Promoting Healthy Life World Bank Group. (2016). Conflict and Violence in the 21ST Century- Current Trends As Observed in Empirical Research and Statistics, World Bank Group. Fragility, Conflict &Violence.

World Health Organization (2000): International guide for monitoring alcohol consumption and related harm. Department of Mental Health and Substance Dependence World Bank. (2006).Health Financing Revisited A Practitioner's Guide.

World Health Organization. (WHO). (2001). The World Health Report 2001— Mental Health: New Understanding, New Hope. Geneva: WHO.

The WHO World Mental Health Survey Consortium. (2004). Prevalence, severity, and unmet need for treatment of mental disorders in the World Health Organization World Mental Health Surveys. *JAMA, 291*, 2581-90.

World Health Organization (WHO). (2004a). Prevention of mental disorders : effective interventions and policy options : summary report / a report of the World Health Organization Dept. of Mental

Health and Substance Abuse ; in collaboration with the Prevention Research Centre of the Universities of Nijmegen and Maastricht

World Health Organization (WHO). (2004b). Developing Health Management Information Systems. A Practical Guide for Developing Countries, p. 3. Geneva: World Health Organization.

World Health Organization (WHO).(2004c).Bulletin of the World Health Organization, Substance use problems in developing countries, Ref. No. 04-016212.

WHO(2004d): Promoting mental health : concepts, emerging evidence, practice : summary report / a report from the World Health Organization, Department of Mental Health and Substance Abuse in collaboration with the Victorian Health Promotion Foundation (VicHealth) and the University of Melbourne

World Health Organization (WHO). (2005). "Atlas: Child and Adolescent Mental Health Resources: Global Concerns: Implications for the Future." Geneva: WHO.

World Health Organization (WHO).(2005b).Strategy on Health Care Financing for Countries of the Western Pacific and South-East Asia Regions (2006–2010).

World Health Organization (WHO). (2007). "Breaking the Vicious Cycle between Mental Ill-Health and Poverty." *Mental Health Core to Development Information Sheet.* Geneva: WHO.

World Health Organization (WHO).(2007b). Employment conditions and health inequality, Final report to the WHO Commission on Social Determinants of Health (CSDH) 2007)

WHO (2017 C). Alcohol and drug use disorders: Global Health Estimates, WHO Forum on alcohol, drugs and addictive behaviours Enhancing public health actions through partnerships and collaboration

World Health Organization (WHO).(2008).Commission on Social Determinants of Health (CSDH), *Closing the gap in a generation: Health equity through action on the social determinants of health: Final report of the Commission on Social Determinants of Health.*

World Health Organization (WHO).(2009).Global health risks: mortality and burden of disease attributable to selected major risks, Retrieved from http:// apps.who.int/iris/bitstre am/10665/44203/1/9789241563871_eng.pdf

World Health Organization (WHO).(2010a).Global Burden of Disease Study 2010: Estimating the burden of disease from drug dependence

World Health Organization (WHO). (2010b). *Mental Health and Development: Targeting People with Mental Health Conditions as a Vulnerable Group.* Geneva: WHO.

World Health Organization (WHO). (2011a). Mental Health Atlas 2011. Retrieved from http://www.who.int/mental_health/publications/ mental_health_atlas_2011/en/

World Health Organization (WHO).(2011b).Global burden of mental disorders and the need for a comprehensive, coordinated response from health and social sectors at the country level Report by the Secretariat, EB130/9 130th session 1 December 2011.

World Health Organization (WHO).(2012a). Risks to Mental Health: An overview of vulnerabilities and Risk Factors. Background Paper by WHO Secretariat for the Development of a Comprehensive Mental health action Plan, Retrieved from http://www.who.int/mental_health/mhgap/risks_to_ mental_health_EN_27_08_12.pdf

World Health Organization (WHO).(2012b). Global burden of mental disorders and the need for a comprehensive, coordinated response from health and social sectors at the country level, Report by the Secretariat, SIXTY-FIFTH WORLD HEALTH ASSEMBLY, A65/10,16 March 2012, provisional agenda item.

World Health Organization (WHO).(2012d).Mental Health Global Action Programme (mhGAP) Close the gap, dare to care, retrieved from http://apps. who.int/iris/bitstream/10665/67222/1/ WHO_NMH_MSD_02.1.pdf

World Health Organization. (2012e). Global burden of disease 2010 study, retrieved from http://www.who.int/pmnch/media/

news/2012/ who_burdenofdisease/en/

World Health Organization (WHO). (2013a). "Mental Health Action Plan 2013–2020"

World Health Organization (WHO). (2013b). "Investing in Mental Health: Evidence for Action"

World Health Organization (WHO). (2013c). "The European Mental Health Action Plan." Regional Committee for Europe, Sixty-third session, Çeşme Izmir, Turkey, 16–19 September 2013 http://www.euro.who.int/ data/ assets/pdf_file/0004/194107/63wd11e_MentalHealth-3.pdf

World Health Organization (WHO).(2013d).Social Determinants of Health

World Health Organization (WHOa). (2014a). "Social Determinants of Mental Health" World Health Organization (WHO). (2014b). Global status report on violence prevention 2014.

World Health Organization (WHO). (2015). Mental Health Atlas2014. Geneva: WHO.

World Health Organization (WHO) and World Organization of Family Doctors (WONCA). (2008). *Integrating Mental Health into Primary Care: A Global Perspective*. Geneva: WHO.

WHO (2016 a): The health and social effects of nonmedical cannabis use

WHO(2016b)Disease burden and mortality estimates, DISEASE BURDEN, 2000–2016

WHO(2017a) Depression and Other Common Mental Disorders: Global Health Estimates. Geneva: World Health Organization; 2017.

World Health Organization (WHO). (2017b). Mental Health Status of Adolescents in South-East Asia: Evidence for Action April, 2017.

WHO ATLAS on substance use (2010) — Resources for the prevention and treatment of substance use disorders

WHO-AIMS Report on Mental Health System in South Africa, WHO and Department of Psychiatry and Mental Health, University of Cape Town, Cape Town, South Africa, 2007).

World Inequality Report. (2018). World Inequality Database, WID. world.

Wilkinson, R. G., &Marmot, M. (Eds). (2003). *Social Determinants of Health: The Solid Facts*. Copenhagen: WHO.

Wittchen, H.-U., Jacobi, F., Rehm, J., Gustavsson, A., Svensson, M., Jönsson, B., ... Steinhausen, H-C. (2011). The Size and Burden of Mental Disorders and Other Disorders of the Brain in Europe. *European Neuro psychopharmacology, 21*, 655–79.

Wyszewianski, L. (2002). Access to Care: Remembering Old Lessons. Health Services Research, 37(6), 1441–1443. doi.org/10.1111/1475-6773.12171

Yates, S. & Payne, M. (2007). Not so NEET? A Critique of the Use of 'NEET' in Setting Targets for Interventions with Young People

Yeniay, O., &Goktas, A. (2002).A Comparison of Partial Least Squares Regres- sion with Other Prediction Methods. *Hacettepe Journal of Mathematics and Statistics, 31*, 99-111.

Yitzhaki, S: 1979, Relative deprivation and the Gini coefficient, Quarterly Journal of Economics 93, pp. 321–324.

Zhao, Q., Caiafa, C. F., Mandic, D. P., Chao, Z. C., Nagasaka, Y., Fujii, N., Zhang, L.,& Cichocki, A. (2013). Higher order partial least squares (HOPLS): a generalized multilinear regression method. Pattern Analysis and Machine Intelligence. *IEEE Transactions,35*(7), 1660–1673.

END NOTES

1. Global Burden of Disease studies split the neuropsychiatric issues into two separate categories: mental and substance-use disorders, and neurological disorders. Conventionally, high-income countries consider neurological disorders separately from mental and substance-use disorders. In this document, most of the data used from WHO follow this convention.

2. One DALY can be thought of as one lost year of "healthy" life. The sum of these DALYs across the population, or the burden of disease, can be thought of as a measurement of the gap between current health status and an ideal health situation where the entire population lives to an advanced age, free of disease and disability. DALYs (disability-adjusted life years) = YLDs (years lived with disability) + YLLs (years of life lost) (Patel et al., 2010; WHO, http://www.who.int/healthinfo/global_burden_disease/metrics_daly/en/). YLD = P × DW where: P = number of prevalent cases, DW = disability weight; YLL=N × L, Where N = number of deaths, L = standard life expectancy at age of death in years

3. Research suggests a reciprocal relationship between socioeconomic status and mental health, although social causation has more evidence (Warren, 2009).

4. As per the World Bank report (July 2015), low-income economies are defined as those with a GNI per capita, calculated using the World Bank Atlas method, of $1,045 or less in 2014; middle-income economies are those with a GNI per capita of more than $1,045 but less than $12,736; high-income econ-

omies are those with a GNI per capita of $12,736 or more. http://blogs.worldbank.org/opendata/new-country-classifications.

5. BRICS countries, is a term used to refer to Brazil, Russia, India, China, and South Africa grouped together as they are all at a newly advanced stage of economic development
6. Prevalence indicates the widespread nature of the disease. Under most circumstances, prevalence = incidence × disease duration. Studies generally report prevalence as the occurrence of disorder in the past 12 months prior to assessment, or sometimes the figure is for a person's lifetime prior to assessment—the so-called lifetime prevalence. Incidence conveys information about the risk of contracting the disease during the specified period. Incidence proportion is expressed as: Number of new cases of disease during specified time interval/ Population at start of time interval. Some empirical studies also report incidence rate as occurrence (first-ever and recurrent) of a disease cases per thousand of population. Prevalence and incidence are two measures of occurrence.
7. Though consistent efforts are being made by international organizations(such as WHO) to strengthen epidemiological research in the international mental health community, the global picture of disorders, however, remains inadequate and underestimate, largely because of two limitations(Baxter et al 2013): (1) highly variable regional coverage, and (2) important methodological issues that prevented synthesis across studies, including the use of varying case definitions, the selection of samples not allowing generalization, lack of standardized indicators, and incomplete reporting.
8. "Mental, and substance use disorders," defined in the GBD 2010 study, are those that conform to diagnostic classifications provided in the Diagnostic and Statistical Manual of Mental Disorders (DSM-IV-TR) and the International Classification of Diseases (ICD- 10). See Table 1 in Whiteford et al. (2015)

9. Depressive disorders include two main sub-categories: depressive episodes (which involve symptoms such as depressed mood, loss of interest and enjoyment, decreased energy), and dysthymia, a persistent or chronic form of mild depression (the symptoms of dysthymia are similar to depressive episode, but tend to be less intense and last longer). (WHO 2017).

10. Anxiety disorders refer to a group of mental disorders characterized by feelings of anxiety and fear, including generalized anxiety disorder, panic disorder, phobias, social anxiety disorder, obsessive-compulsive disorder and post-traumatic stress disorder (WHO, 2017).

11. As pointed out by Whiteford et al. (2013), the growth of the burden of mental and substance-use disorders between 1990 and 2010 for most disorders was driven by population growth and aging.

12. WHO (2017): Mental health of older adults 12 December 2017, Information Page, https://www.who.int/news-room/fact-sheets/detail/mental-health-of-older-adults

13. Comorbidity describes two or more disorders or illnesses occurring in the same person. They can occur at the same time or one after the other.(NIDA. (2018, August 1).

14. Multiple sources define the age group of adolescents and youth differently. National Survey on Drug Use and Health (NSDUH) (2014) defines "youth" as ages 12–17, young adults as ages 18–25, and adults 26+. Substance Abuse and Mental Health Services Administration, Results from the 2013 National Survey on Drug Use and Health (2014): Summary of National Findings, NSDUH Series H-48, HHS Publication No. (SMA) 14-4863.

15. Longitudinal studies employ continuous or repeated measures to follow particular individuals (cohorts) over different time intervals.

16. Social capital can be defined as "networks together with shared norms, values and understandings that facilitate co-operation within or among groups"(Keeley 2007).

17. Shlomo Yitzhaki (1979) operationalized relative deprivation by measuring the average difference between a person's income and the incomes of all individuals with a higher income in that person's reference group. A central idea of Yitzhaki's formulation is that individuals tend to weigh upward comparisons more heavily than downward comparisons. Empirical studies in the USA generally reported evidence in support of the hypothesis that relative deprivation associated with increased risks of mortality, mental health services utilization, and poor self-rated health (Eibner and Evans 2005; Eibner, Sturn, and Gresenz 2004).

18. $Q_2 = 1 - \frac{PRESS}{\Sigma(y_1 - \bar{y})}$, where $PRESS = \Sigma(y_1 - \hat{y})^2$ = Predicted Residual Sum of Squares, and $\Sigma(y_1 - \bar{y})^2$ is the total sum of squares (TSS). The smaller the PRESS, better it is from predictability point of view.

19. The VIP value is a weighted sum of squares of the PLS weights, which takes into account the explained variance of each PLS dimension.

20. Piketty's reasoning can be represented as follows. From the view point of functional income distribution, a country's national income is composed of the share of labor and share of capital. The share of capital income (rents, dividends, interest, and realized capital gains) has increased significantly in the past two decades. The share of capital can be written as, a=r x β where r=rate of return on capital, and β the capital income ratio (the capital stock/the annual glow of income) (Piketty, see Doody [2015] Piketty on capital and inequality).The course of wealth distribution in a country depends on wealth accumulation, wealth concentration, and inheritance of family assets. To explain wealth accumulation out of earned income, Piketty posits a dynamic law relating to capital/income ratio, β, to economy's savings rate() and growth rate(g) as follows $\beta = \frac{s}{g}$(Harrod-Domar-Solow wealth-income ratio [capital income ratio]), where s is the savings rate and g is the growth rate (including both real per capita and population growth) (Alverodo et al. 2013). If a country that saves a lot and grows

slowly will over a long run, it will accumulate an enormous stock of capital. Picketty argues that if rate of return on capital, r, remains significantly above the growth rate, g, for extended period of time, then the risk of divergence in the distribution of wealth is very high (citation by Doody 2015). As pointed out by Solow (P 3) on his comments on Piketty's book, "Income from wealth is probably even more concentrated than wealth itself because, as Piketty notes, large blocks of wealth tend to earn a higher return than small ones." Income from work is naturally less concentrated than income from wealth (Solow 2014). The inheritance of wealth is very important factor in explaining lifetime income inequality. The joint distribution of earned income and capital income show that the same people are at the top of both the distribution (Alverdo et al 2013). Because capital is often transferred via inheritance, Piketty worries that capitalism naturally tends toward patrimonial capitalism (given r>g, Alverdo et al). In the future, much of the wealth will be inherited rather than earned. People with inherited wealth need save only a portion of their income from capital to see that capital grow more quickly than the economy as a whole (Alverdo et al. 2013). Effect of wealth concentration on income inequalities can further be elaborated by combining Piketty's analysis and Gini's decomposition for two factor model. Combining the above information with Gini decomposition for two factor model (see Jacobson and Occhino 2012b), Gini index = labor's share of income × concentration index of labor income + capital's share of income × concentration index of capital income, it can, thus, be seen that Gini index will increase, showing greater inequalities in income, as the last term increase.

21. Vives et al. (2013), analyzing the association between precarious employment and poor mental health , constructed an employment precariousness index using six dimensions of employment- encompassing contractual features of precarious employment and workplace social dimensions of employment relationships. The dimensions reflecting contractual aspects of

the contract are employment instability (type and duration of the contract), low wages (and possible economic deprivation), limited worker rights and social protection, and individualized contracts (individual-level bargaining over employment conditions).

22. EPL is a measure of employment protection strictness, and it is constructed on a scale from 0 to 6, with the higher scores reflecting stricter regulation. The issues of "hiring and firing" are deemed an inherent part of EPL.

23. Ecological analyses look at the health of populations, not of individuals. In these types of studies, researchers examine the health of a population before and after some time-specific event, like after large public health interventions.

24. Epidemiology is the study of how often diseases occur in different groups of people and why.

25. The DSM 5 recognizes substance-related disorders resulting from the use of 10 separate classes of drugs: alcohol; caffeine; cannabis; hallucinogens (phencyclidine or similarly acting arylcyclohexylamines, and other hallucinogens, such as LSD); inhalants; opioids; sedatives, hypnotics, or anxiolytics; stimulants (including amphetamine-type substances, cocaine, and other stimulants); tobacco; and other or unknown substances. McLellan (2017) has arrayed substances into seven classes based on their pharmacological and behavioral effects:

26. Nicotine — cigarettes, vapor-cigarettes, cigars, chewing tobacco, and snuff

27. Alcohol — including all forms of beer, wine, and distilled liquors

28. Cannabinoids — Marijuana, hashish, hash oil, and edible cannabinoids

29. Opioids — Heroin, methadone, buprenorphine, Oxycodone, Vicodin, and Lortab

30. Depressants — Benzodiazepines (e.g., Valium, Librium, and Xanax) and Barbiturates (e.g., Seconal)

31. Stimulants — Cocaine, amphetamine, methamphetamine, methylphenidate (e.g., Ritalin), and atomoxetine (e.g., Stratera)

32. Hallucinogens — LSD, mescaline, and MDMA (e.g., Ecstasy)

33. The Sociodemographic Index (SDI) is a summary measure of a geography's sociodemographic development. It is based on average income per person, educational attainment, and total fertility rate (TFR). SDI contains an interpretable scale: zero represents the lowest income per capita, lowest educational attainment, and highest TFR observed across all GBD geographies from 1980 to 2015, and one represents the highest income per capita, highest educational attainment, and lowest TFR. The SDI is the geometric mean of total fertility rate, income per capita, and mean years of education among individuals aged 15 years and older, which was included as a composite measure of developmental status in GBD 2016. Global Burden of Disease Collaborative Network. Global Burden of Disease Study 2015 (GBD 2015) Socio-Demographic Index (SDI) 1980–2015. Seattle, United States: Institute for Health Metrics and Evaluation (IHME), 2016.

34. Context conditions include macroeconomic policies, public provision of health, education policies, antipoverty programs, welfare state policies (equal opportunities, housing, social insurance programs), child development programs, and redistribution policies.

35. Based on the survey responses of 707 American adults, Smith (2016) found that the institutional betrayal (negative medical experiences) was reported by two-thirds of the participants. The most common experiences were being prescribed an unnecessary medication (28% of participants), being given an incorrect diagnosis (27%), not being notified of test results (24.6%), having an allergic reaction to medication (24.5%), and undergoing an unnecessary procedure or test (22.5%). (Smith 2016)

36. This is a statement of a psychiatrist, Dr. Brock Chisholm, the first Director-General of the World Health Organization (WHO).

37. Even including prenatal, pregnancy, and perinatal periods (WHO 2014a).

Printed in Great Britain
by Amazon